DESTRUCTION, DEATH . . . AND LINGERING QUESTIONS

• *It looked like a town torn by war:* Rows of burned-out houses; a huge, gaping crater; debris scattered for miles. . . . and bodies everywhere, some still attached to their seats.

• *Meet Ella Ramsden, Lockerbie's "luckiest survivor":* Seventy bodies were recovered from the wreckage of her home. Yet, she walked away unscathed with her dog, Cara.

• *The warnings:* Did authorities act properly in withholding reports of advance bomb threats?

• *Air security:* How bad is it? What systems did Pan Am use? Can airports and air travel *ever* be made safe? Could the Lockerbie disaster have been prevented?

• *Who is the leading suspect?* The author's sources point to terrorist Ahmad Jabril. Learn why and how he was implicated, and who were his accomplices.

• *The undercover investigation:* Was the CIA's presence connected to the bombing? Did American authorities really know the identity of the perp[...]e crash?

D1413685

LOCKERBIE
THE TRAGEDY OF FLIGHT 103

David Johnston

ST. MARTIN'S PRESS/NEW YORK

Photo credits: Jim Galloway, *Glasgow Herald,* Insert pages 1, 3, 4: *Scottish Sun,* Insert pages 2, 5: Tom Stoddart, Insert pages 6, 7, 8.

This book was first published in Great Britain by Bloomsbury Publishing Limited, with the title *Lockerbie—The Real Story.*

Published by arrangement with Bloomsbury Publishing Limited

LOCKERBIE: THE TRAGEDY OF FLIGHT 103

ISBN: 0-312-92212-4

Printed in the United States of America

First St. Martin's Press mass market edition/November 1989

10 9 8 7 6 5 4 3 2 1

CONTENTS

INTRODUCTION

At three minutes past seven on Wednesday, 21 December 1988, a bomb exploded in the forward cargo hold of a Pan Am Boeing 747, 31,000 feet above Lockerbie, Scotland. Two hundred seventy people died in what had become Britain's worst ever air disaster.

In the weeks that followed the Lockerbie air disaster, the grief of relatives of those who had died turned slowly to anger as it became clear that their loved ones need not have died. They were victims of the complacency, incompetence, and bureaucracy that had conspired to allow a bomb on the unchecked aircraft at a time when the aviation industry had been told not only that a bomb attack on an aircraft was likely, but also what sort of bomb to look out for.

The story of the Lockerbie disaster is one of supreme importance for anyone who ever steps onto an aircraft, and, as eleven people from the quiet Scottish town learned, for anyone who lives under commercial flight paths. Much of the story is still to come. Much is revealed here for the first time. The inescapable conclusion is that air security does not need governmental tinkering to safe-guard passengers; it does need a complete restructuring and a higher priority placed on it by the airlines, and all others concerned.

I would like to thank all who have helped in the compilation of *Lockerbie: The Tragedy of Flight 103*. During the writing of this book, I have been given widespread and unique cooperation from official sources. Many have also risked their careers out of desire for the truth of Lockerbie to be known. To protect them, some of their names have been changed in this book.

The only entity that has been unwilling to help has been Pan Am itself. The airline declined to be interviewed. They asked instead for a list of written questions to be submitted. After six weeks and many phone calls, their answers arrived, and are reproduced here as an appendix; readers can judge for themselves whether these answers are adequate.

David Johnston
Edinburgh, May 1989

1

LOCKERBIE,
DECEMBER 21, 1988

"It got louder and louder and the whole house started
to shake."

Ella Ramsden was depressed.

The weekend before Christmas her family had been
together for the first time in three and a half years. They
had celebrated the holiday a week early, and then, on
Wednesday, her son Ian and his wife and two young sons
had left Mrs. Ramsden's neat council home in Lockerbie
to begin their journey home to West Germany. That had
left the slightly built fifty-nine-year-old widow as she usually was—alone, with Cara, her Jack Russell, and the
budgie and three goldfish.

Mrs. Ramsden had tidied up the mess inevitably cre-
ated by two boisterous youngsters, made her tea, and sat
down for the first time that day to watch Scottish Television's soap, *Take the High Road*. It was not until the program ended at seven o'clock that she got around to
opening that day's delivery of Christmas cards.

"I just got down on my knees in front of the fire," she
says, smiling nervously, "when I heard this terrible noise. I
still can't describe it. It got louder and louder and the

whole house started to shake. I turned to the dog and said, 'There's something far wrong here, Cara.' " Still on her knees, Mrs. Ramsden moved across to the window of her living room and opened the curtains. From there, high up on the east side of the town, she could see the whole area lit up with a fierce light. It was everywhere.

"There was a terrific explosion. It was like the old pictures of the atom bomb. I knew something terrible had happened. I thought it was one of those low-flying planes had crashed carrying a bomb."

It was 7:05 P.M. on Wednesday, 21 December 1988. The luckiest day of Ella Ramsden's life.

"I said to Cara, 'We'd better get out.' She was on the sofa beside me. I picked her up and moved to the back door on the other side of the house from the blast.

"When I got into the kitchen, the door would not open. It had been jammed with the explosion, and as I struggled with it, the lights all went out. I wondered if the rug which sits at the door had got behind it to stop it from opening. I bent down to try and move it, and as I straightened up again, the whole house started to shake.

"I held on to the handle of the door with one hand, Cara with the other, and the house began to shake again . . . this time much more violently. I remember a terrible whooshing noise.

"I was being sucked back into the house. My legs were hurting as dust and dirt were sucked in past me. I think it was only the weight of Cara on my arm that stopped me being drawn back as well.

"All of a sudden, when I thought my last moments had come—I really did think they had come—it stopped.

Then there was a terrible quietness which I will never forget.

"I looked up, and from where I was standing, I could see the sky and the stars. I thought: I've got to get out of here. I was frightened to move, I was frightened to let Cara down, in case she ran away. I reached into a cupboard and pulled out a pan. I gave the door an almighty whack and it smashed.

"Even when I stuck my head out of the door, there was still this silence, nobody, no noise. I started shouting for my neighbors, Martha and John, but they were away, out, unknown to me. I was shouting: 'Please come and get my wee dog, please come and help me.' "

One of the neighbors had gone to the front of Mrs. Ramsden's home, the last house in Park Place. It had collapsed. The gable end had gone. Rubble had piled up in the garden. Only a short section of roof protruded from the house next door. There was a large section of what appeared to be a plane's fuselage lying in the side garden, where Mrs. Ramsden's late husband had once grown show chrysanthemums that had been the envy of the town. The neighbor told his family that their friend must be dead. There was no way anyone could have survived. But then her shouts were heard and the neighbor ran with two others to the back.

Mrs. Ramsden says: "When they saw me, one really let rip—'She's alive, she's fucking alive,' he shouted. I made him promise not to let Cara go, then handed her over, then they helped me out over the rubble."

The rescuers and the rescued scrambled up the grass

bank at the back of the house. In the road that runs along the back, a body lay motionless.

Mrs. Ramsden looked at her devastated home and silently thanked God that her family had left earlier that day. Her grandson's bedroom was gone. Shocked and shaking, she turned her back on her house and was led away to her brother's home on the other side of town.

In the darkness she would not have seen that on the few remaining slates of what had once been her roof, a body lay spread-eagled and battered. In the days that followed, seventy other bodies would be dug out of the rubble of her home. Ella Ramsden was the luckiest survivor of the Lockerbie air disaster.

Fifty miles away, in the town of Ayr, all hell broke out at the telephone exchange, the main one serving southwest Scotland. The emergency lines jammed as Lockerbie residents who still had telephone service, and others from miles around, dialed 999, Scotland's emergency number.

As Ella Ramsden was struggling to get out of what had been her home, the rest of her neighbors in the Park Plaza housing estate had come out of their houses and, using flashlights, were discovering a scene of devastation. Few bodies were visible, but wreckage lay everywhere and the gale force southwesterly wind was carrying reams of paperwork, letters, postcards, and money.

Two terraces of houses stretch out in front of Park Place, separated by wide gardens. The back windows of Margaret Cameron's home look out on Mrs. Ramsden's garden. They had blown in. Her kitchen had been filled with earth sent flying by the impact of the section of the plane that had landed in Mrs. Ramsden's garden. Mixed up in it were scores of airline knives and forks. Her garden was covered in paper and money. Many thousands of dollars had blown up against her fence. In the mess of her kitchen Mrs. Cameron found two half-written postcards and a jar of makeup.

"I had been upstairs getting ready to go out to bingo," says Mrs. Cameron. "I remember thinking how awful the wind was when I heard the sound of a low-flying jet. It's something we've become used to here over the years. But instead of going away again, the noise of this plane just got louder and louder.

"I actually thought it was going to hit the house, and started running downstairs. As I reached the hall, my husband grabbed me and pushed me up against the wall. He said, 'It's an earthquake.'

"I opened the front door and we went outside. As we reached the doorstep, there was a huge explosion across the town. I could feel the heat on my face. It was searing, like putting your face right in front of a blazing fire.

"I thought, My God, the petrol station's blown up."

What Mrs. Cameron was referring to is the Townfoot Filling Station which lies on the main road through Lockerbie, down from Rosebank, across the railway tracks on the west side of the town. In fact, the blast had come from behind the gas station—Sherwood Crescent.

There, the wings containing the jumbo jet's fuel tanks had crashed to earth on top of the neat bungalows that border the main A74 road between Scotland and England. The explosion that followed sent a fireball three hundred feet into the air and gouged a huge crater into the earth where, seconds before, stood numbers 13 and 16 Sherwood Crescent.

At 7:03 there was only one policeman in Lockerbie. Superintendent John Carpenter was sitting in the living room of his Sherwood Crescent home watching television when he heard an almighty roar in the night sky. He leapt out of his chair just as the wings containing twenty thousand gallons of aviation fuel exploded in Sherwood Crescent.

Seventy-five-year-old John Smith and his wife Janet, seventy-four, lived just a few yards from the center of that blast. The roar had at first drowned out the quiet clinking of Mrs. Smith's knitting needles. Like so many others, they thought it was a low-flying jet. Mr. Smith says: "I was just about to say, 'This one's very low,' but I never got the words out, because I heard a big bang. It hit the roof of the house.

"Immediately the house was on fire from the petrol. I ran to the back door. I couldn't get near it for flames. I ran to the bedroom. It was the same there."

Mr. Smith eventually fought his way out through the flames and into their front garden. His wife was still inside. She had collapsed on the floor. He went back into the inferno and—he still can't remember how—managed to stumble back outside with his wife.

"We just took it step by step and didn't panic. We got out of the house, onto the steps, then had to try and avoid the flames in the garden. I had fallen, and by the time we reached the garden wall, I was done . . . We both shouted for help, and someone came running over from the neighbors."

* * *

Farther around the Crescent, Mrs. Sarah Lawson had just phoned her sister in Canada. She too was going to play bingo that night, but first she thought she'd see who was the guest on *This Is Your Life.*

As Michael Aspèl pulled out the big red book on veteran puppeteer Harry Corbett, Lossie (as she is known throughout the town) heard that terrible noise of what she too thought was a low-flying jet. But in Sherwood Crescent the intensity of noise was bad enough to split eardrums. "Then it went quiet. A few seconds later there was a tremendous bang." Lossie leapt from her armchair and ran to the front door. Stones and boulders began to rain down on her home. Frozen with terror, she stood at the front door for a few seconds. Then she ran back into the living room to get a coat. A huge boulder crashed through the roof and landed right on the chair where she'd been sitting a few seconds earlier.

"I managed to get my coat and put it on, and just then a man came to the door. I don't know who he was, but he said, 'You'd better get out in case the houses go on fire.' I went out onto the street and, up the road, houses were on fire. Two or three neighbors came out of their homes . . . they were all pretty shocked."

As air replaced the smoke generated by the blazing kerosene, the heat of the explosion was so fierce that within yards of the blast anything that could burn, burst into flames. Houses, hedges, and garden sheds were engulfed in flames that lit up the whole area.

The local Church of Scotland minister, the Reverend Jim Annand, had run out of Dryfesdale Manse just around the corner from Sherwood Crescent. He thought that the fierce crackling sounds he heard were bullets exploding from what he presumed to be a crashed fighter. He says that in those few seconds of destruction, many of the older residents of the area were taken back in their minds to the blitzes of the Second World War.

"One woman told me that, as she was running out of her home, she actually stopped in the hallway and started looking for the tin hat she'd thrown out in 1946. For those few terrible seconds, she had left the 1980s and gone back to the war."

All around the town the smell of aviation fuel hung in the air, most intensely around the houses of Sherwood Crescent. Flaming debris had set fire to tires at the rear of the gas station. Thick, black smoke filled the air and sent the stench of burning rubber over the town.

On the A74 road, drivers speeding along could only stare in disbelief as wreckage showered across the roadway.

In the newly built garage of his Sherwood Crescent home, David Edward and fourteen-year-old Stephen Flannigan were repairing Stephen's sister's bike. It was the first day of the school vacation, and Stephen had decided to fix the puncture that had kept ten-year-old Joanne's bicycle off the road. He had been bored most of the day, tidying up his bedroom at number 16 and listening to Dire Straits.

Stephen said (as reported in the *Daily Mail*) that his mother, his sister Joanne, and he had had tea together, and then he had gone to see David Edward, who was good with bikes and had said he'd help. It hadn't taken long to fix the bike, because there wasn't a puncture, the tire was just flat. After pumping it up, David had been about to put it back on when Stephen heard a rumbling like thunder away in the distance. David said, "What's that?" and Stephen said, "It's thunder." Then the strip light in the garage started falling off the ceiling. Stephen became a bit concerned, thinking, If that's thunder, I've never heard anything like it.

Looking through the garage doors, Stephen could see small pieces of wreckage crashing from the sky. Then he knew it was a plane. David said, "Come on, let's get out of here." The whole garage had begun to shake.

When they came out, Stephen had still not given a thought to his own house. Then they saw an elderly couple running across the road from the house opposite. It was on fire.

The woman had no shoes on and her feet had been burnt. David and Stephen took the couple behind the garage, where there was some shelter. The woman kept saying, "Have you got a pair of shoes?" Then she said she was cold, and Stephen gave her his jacket. They could see houses far away where there were lights on, and they told the couple to go and knock on the door of one of those.

A house nearby, where Mrs. Mary Lancaster lived, was burning. David, axe in hand, went to break in. The flames were getting higher, and Stephen, believing that his neighbor was already dead, kept telling David, "It's no use. You'll be killed if you go any further." Finally convinced, David instead went into his house and got a big pile of coats for his now-homeless neighbors. His own family were out delivering Christmas presents.

* * *

About this time, on the other side of Scotland, the RAF's main search-and-rescue headquarters at Pitreavie Castle in Fife was beginning to get calls from reporters checking out police reports of an air crash at Lockerbie.

The duty officer was able to give only the briefest of details. A 747 jet had been lost from radar screens at three minutes past seven, shortly after crossing the Scottish border. The controller told reporters that he understood that it was a New York–bound flight from London Heathrow.

By 7:35 journalists were being told the plane that had disappeared was Pan Am Flight 103, with 276 people on board. The figure would later be amended to 259, when airline staff realized that the plane's crew had been counted twice.

A few miles away from Lockerbie, in Dumfries, the main town of the region, Chief Constable John Boyd was puttering around in his home. The television was on in the background but he was paying little attention. Then at the end of *Coronation Street*, Independent Television News flashed the news: a jumbo jet had crashed on a gas station in Lockerbie, twenty-five miles north of Carlisle, and it was understood that there were many casualties.

Chief Constable Boyd says: "A couple of minutes later the force control room phoned me to say what had happened. I realized I would not be home for at least the next forty-eight hours. I put on my uniform and went to police headquarters."

Mr. Boyd drove away from his home that night unaware that his force, the smallest in Scotland, had that

night been delivered the largest murder hunt the world
has ever seen.

Within minutes of the explosion, fire, police, and ambulance controls realized they were dealing with a major incident. Every available emergency vehicle was directed to
Lockerbie with the utmost speed. From having just one
policeman in the town at seven P.M., numbers built up
minute by minute, to culminate within hours in a huge
presence of emergency workers, possibly the biggest since
wartime. As they arrived in Lockerbie, there was a feeling
of helplessness, disbelief, and shock. The flames from
scores of fires in Sherwood Crescent lit the night sky. By
midnight Lockerbie was in total chaos.

The Dumfries & Galloway emergency plan for a major incident had been set in motion. It had been designed
with the possibility of a nuclear accident at the region's
Chapelcross Power Station in mind. It was being implemented for the previously unthinkable—a jumbo jet crashing on Lockerbie.

Chief Constable John Boyd had telephoned neighboring chief constables, and hundreds of extra police were
being drafted into the area. Medical teams from all over
Scotland—and as far as Humberside—were making their
way to the town.

Hospitals across west Scotland were put on emergency standby and were prepared to treat what was feared
to be hundreds of casualties. In the end, only twelve people, all from the Sherwood Crescent area, needed hospital
treatment.

Communications were virtually nonexistent. People

were wandering the streets of the town, dazed and unable to decide what to do next. By ten P.M. a list of crash "survivors" was being drawn up at the town hall. One by one residents of the affected areas of the town were registering with police.

Reporters trying to make their way to Lockerbie found the main roads to town completely blocked with traffic that had ground to a halt. As deadlines loomed large, some abandoned their cars and ran for three or four miles past the lines of stationary vehicles.

I was lucky enough to be driven by a resident of the area. We approached the town along backroads and farm tracks. From high up on the Moffat hills to the west of the town, the flashing blue lights of scores of emergency vehicles could be seen through the darkness. As we neared the town center and passed the golf club, we could see helicopters taking off and landing—they were the yellow Sea Kings and Wessexes of the RAF's Search and Rescue Squadron, flying personnel to various points around the town, using their powerful searchlights to try and discover the extent of the disaster, how far the wreckage had spread.

A large crowd of people had gathered around the town hall, where attempts were being made to account for the residents of the affected area. Some residents had fled their homes in panic, while others had died. The main street was cluttered with ambulances, fire engines, army jeeps and personnel carriers. There were several of what looked to be a mountain rescue team, complete with sturdy boots, woolen socks, and heavy anoraks. There were also police and RAF dog handlers. Among the townsfolk were reporters, most of them called out from their homes or from pubs. There were stories everywhere. As I walked up the main street, past the police station, the road was increasingly littered with debris, and small stones made walking difficult. The Sherwood housing estate off to the left was a center of activity. Police guarded the only road into the estate, refusing to let anyone past. It was, however, still possible to get up to the scene of greatest devastation. Through the gardens, climbing over fences, the grass began to feel crispy underfoot: it had been scorched by the intense heat of the blast a few hours before.

Court official Iain Scott spends weekdays away from his home in Lockerbie's Annandale Terrace, living near his Edinburgh job with relatives in the Scottish capital. On seeing news of the disaster on television, and unable to get through by telephone, he'd jumped into his car and driven the sixty miles to Lockerbie.

After making sure that his family was all right, Mr. Scott joined the large group of people at the town hall at the top of Lockerbie's main street. A policeman was at the front door assuring townsfolk, where he could, that their friends and relatives were accounted for.

Near the front of the throng, Mr. Scott saw Stephen Flannigan. He was friendly with Stephen's father and mother, Tom and Kath, and knew Stephen and his sister well.

"Stephen asked the policeman, 'Is there any news of the Flannigans?' I think we realized by then that there was no hope for Tom, Kath, and Joanne, but the policeman looked at his list and said Mrs. Flannigan was registered alive.

"You could see Stephen's eyes brighten up. Then when people said they did not think that possible, the policeman looked at his list again. It had been a mistake. It was, in fact, a reference to Stephen himself. The list had been badly written and Mr. S. Flannigan looked like Mrs. Flannigan.

"Tom's friend, Bill Harley, put his arm around Stephen and led him across the road from the town hall, where Bill lived in a flat above his garage."

Many people whose houses had been damaged by the falling aircraft left their homes to stay with friends and relatives in the town. Others, just a few, were given temporary accommodation organized by a team of social workers that had begun arriving at the town hall within minutes of the disaster.

Very quickly, police commanders came to the conclusion that there could have been no survivors from the plane. They checked as best they could in the rubble of Sherwood Crescent and in the devastation of the Rosebank area, and established that there were no passengers or crew alive.

Among the medical teams driven and flown to Lockerbie that night was Dr. Keith Little, senior consultant at Edinburgh Royal Infirmary's accident and emergency department, and a veteran of many years of treating casualties of road carnage. Despite being flown to Lockerbie in an RAF Wessex rescue helicopter, he had, in fact, arrived later than other doctors from his hospital who'd been driven by police. His helicopter had had to battle against the gales as it crossed the higher border hills, landing him in Lockerbie just after ten P.M.

"We had no idea what to expect. We were told a jumbo jet had landed on Lockerbie, and just assumed there would be lots of casualties. We presumed there would be little chance of survivors from the aircraft itself, but anticipated a lot of ground casualties.

"When we arrived, after reporting to police, the medical staff were split up and went 'round to what police had established to be six main crash sites. We were checking that there were no viable casualties, and there were not. All we had was a lot of wreckage and a lot of bodies.

"By midnight all the crash sites had been checked. We met other medical teams from Newcastle and Humberside and assured them there was nothing to be done, and they turned 'round and went home again.

"The communications all this time were appalling. I had a handheld telephone, but the lines were all blocked by the increasingly large numbers of reporters that had descended on the town."

Dr. Little and his colleagues then set off back to Edinburgh, only to be recalled just ten miles from the north of the town and asked to help by going around the scene again and putting identification labels on the various bodies or parts of bodies that had been found. Chief Constable Boyd had decided from the outset that there was always a chance that the disaster would turn into a criminal investigation, and he ordered that every body should be treated as a potential murder victim. Under Scottish law, this entailed the laborious task of noting the exact position of what had been found and where. In the chaos,

teams of officers had been detailed, as well as possible in
the dark, to cordon off each area of wreckage and bodies
to ensure that nothing was disturbed. Small brown labels
bearing the legend DEAD on one side and with room for
noting further details on the other were tied to each body
found.

Dr. Little says: "I was in the Sherwood Crescent area,
and we only had one body, the inhabitant of one of the
houses, by appearance, who had died of severe burns.

"Surrounding that whole area was a mass of bits—I
mean pieces of human anatomy in a variety of shapes and
sizes. Initially we identified what was probably human and
which piece of anatomy it was.

"It became obvious as we went on that this was a
foolish exercise. It was the middle of the night, gale-force
wind, pouring rain, and [we were] working with handheld
torches [flashlights]. We suggested to the police just to seal
the whole area off and wait till daylight."

Shortly after he began examining the bodies that
were found on the first night of the disaster, it was obvious
to Dr. Little that there had been some sort of midair explosion.

"When I was in the Sherwood Crescent area, the
street was littered with pieces, and the field behind the
Crescent was scattered with pieces of human bodies. They
were totally destroyed. Reduced to four- and six-inch
pieces. Some of them had burns, some had not. These
pieces had fallen from a great height and actually had
impacted into the ground, so [the bodies] had not been
destroyed on impact.

"They had been disintegrated into small pieces a long

way up. Some of them were wrapped 'round metal work, some had metal embedded in them. In my limited experience of these matters, it looked as if there had been a major explosion high up and the pieces had just rained down.

"Away from Sherwood the bodies were more intact. They had again obviously fallen from a great height and suffered further damage on impact. They had formed craters in the earth where they fell, obviously at the terminal velocity for a body."

Pathologists have since concluded the passengers on Flight 103 would have died instantly from the depressurization of the plane: "Total decompression will disrupt the anatomy of the body, in particular, parts of the body that are soft, which are fluid- or air-containing. If you have a balloon and you suddenly take the pressure off, the balloon just goes bang. So you're talking about blood vessels, stomach, lungs, possibly heart, head. So the chances of anyone regaining consciousness after decompression must be nil."

Dr. Little says that when he arrived in Lockerbie, he found a totally chaotic situation. There appeared to be little, if any, control. That, he says, is understandable. It was an unforeseeable event which had spread debris over great distances.

In the hours after the crash, the increasing number of police and other emergency workers were sent out in an ever-widening circle around the town. Seemingly no matter how far they went, more wreckage and more bodies were found.

Three miles from the town, along the main road to

the neighboring community of Langholm, a farmer had found the entire cockpit section of the jumbo jet lying in a grass field. It was just over a dry-stone wall from the small parish church at Tundergarth. This stands on the crest of one of the smaller hills in the area, surrounded by its neat graveyard, and beyond are just a few cottages and a substantial farmhouse.

Three miles farther, at Carruthers Farm, Chris Graham found the fields surrounding his farmhouse littered with luggage. It had formed a trail, beginning at the creek that flows past his back door and stretching far up the hill where his sheep graze.

2

FLIGHT 103

"As the bodies fell, the force of the air rushing past
ripped the clothes off their limbs."

In the sticky heat of a New York summer, Chris and Judy
Papadopolous were spending the Independence Day holiday lazing in the garden of their Long Island home. In the
corner of the patio outside their expensive stone-built
house in Lawrence, a television was on in the background.
It did not interrupt the conversation until the evening
news bulletin came on. Chris Papadopolous, like so many
Americans that Fourth of July, was deeply worried about
events in the Gulf. The day before, the cruiser *Vincennes*
had shot down a commercial Iranian airbus over the Strait
of Hormuz in what appeared to be a major blunder. One
of the crew of the *Vincennes*, commanded by Captain Will
Rogers III, had spotted the airbus on his ship's radar but
had mistaken it for an Iranian F14 fighter plane. The aircraft and its 290 passengers had been blown out of the
sky. The television news reported that Rogers had signaled
the Pentagon, saying: "This is a burden I will carry with
me for the rest of my life, but I did what I had to do to
protect my ship and the lives of my crew." He accepted
full responsibility for what he called "this tragic mistake."

President Reagan was on the bulletins too, apologizing for the shooting down of the airbus and offering his condolences to the relatives of those who had died. The President emphasized that, while it had been an accident, he stood by Rogers and said the commander had been right to interpret what had been seen on the *Vincennes'* radar as a potential attack on his ship.

The airbus had been on a short hop from Iran to Mecca, taking 290 pilgrims to their most holy place for the main religious festival of the year. It was Id Al-Adha, the feast day marking the end of the pilgrimage season, the only day on which many poor Islamic families eat meat in the entire year. The airbus had deposited its human cargo into the Strait just four days before the feast. Sixty-six children were among the dead.

Chris Papadopolous was proud of his adopted country. He had been born in Greece and his family still lived there, but he had moved to the United States and, with Judy, built up a successful shoe-importing business.

As Reagan finished speaking on television that night, Chris turned to his wife and said, "You know, I'm beginning to lose it for Reagan. These people are going to get us. Our country has made a very big error here, a very big error."

That is a prophecy that still haunts Judy Papadopolous, now a widow. Her husband died 31,000 feet above Lockerbie, Scotland, four days before Christmas.

She says Chris, because of his birth, had an understanding for what she calls "these people." She believes that she is a widow today as a direct result of Captain Rogers' decision to fire the *Vincennes'* missiles.

* * *

It's lunchtime on December 21 at Old Tappan High School, Riverdale, New Jersey. It's the last day of the term, and the school's administrators are having a quiet pre-Christmas cocktail party. The phone rings. It's a call for Bert Ammerman, the school's former history teacher, now vice-principal. As he goes to pick up the phone, Ammerman thinks to himself, How odd to get a call. No one knows he is at the little gathering.

It was his sister-in-law Carolyn, to say that Bert's brother, Tom, appeared to have been in some kind of a plane accident, could he go to his mother's house right away? Bert and Tom's father had died that summer, and Carolyn Ammerman was worried what the effect of this news might have on her mother-in-law.

Tom Ammerman was an executive with the Saudi Arabian national shipping company. He should not have been on that plane. He was booked on a lunchtime flight, but his office switched him to Pan Am Flight 103 so he could attend one more meeting in London before flying home for Christmas.

The Boeing 747 clipper *Maid of the Seas* that Tom Ammerman and 258 other passengers and crew were boarding at Heathrow airport that Wednesday night would fly the second leg of a flight that was to have gone on to Detroit, Michigan, having originated in Frankfurt, West Germany. The first leg had been flown in a different aircraft, a Boeing 727, with some passengers getting off in London, others going through to New York and Detroit.

The Frankfurt flight had carried U.S. service personnel leaving American bases in West Germany to go home for Christmas: some were traveling alone, some had their whole families—families such as Joe and Dedera Woods and their children, Joe Junior, two, and Chelsea, ten months. Khaled Jafaar, traveling on his own, had flown into Frankfurt that day after visiting relatives in his native Lebanon. He was now returning to his father's home in Detroit.

Three of the Frankfurt passengers would have been keeping themselves to themselves. Dan O'Connor, Ron Lariviere, and Charles McKee were going back to Washington after a more-than-sensitive operation in the Middle East.

There had been 109 people on the flight from Frankfurt, which had left that busy airport on time at four-fifty P.M. The flight was still on time as it taxied to a halt at Pier 7 in Heathrow's Terminal 3. There was plenty of time for the Pan Am baggage handlers to put the cargo of people finishing their flight in London onto the conveyor belt and unload the baggage of the forty-nine passengers transferring to the *Maid of the Seas* parked at the next pier. The transfer baggage was manhandled out of the compartment and placed, item by item, in a cargo container from the jumbo and stored in the forward cargo hold.

Flight 103 was boarded on time and its passengers took their seats. Many may have thought it fortunate that the plane was only three-quarters full; there would be room to stretch out during the flight to New York's John F. Kennedy Airport.

The jumbo was late leaving the terminal. It should have taken off at six P.M. London time, but as takeoff time came, the aircraft remained parked. Eventually the flight did take off, at 6:25, no doubt relieving tension among some of the passengers who saw evening reunions and meetings being put farther and farther back.

As the aircraft, under the control of Captain Jim MacQuarrie, climbed through the heavy cloud above London that December evening, it was heading for the northern corridor up the west coast of Britain into Scotland, and then westward out over the Atlantic. The strong winds that night had determined the flight plan for the crew.

MacQuarrie was a pilot's pilot in every way. His flying and leadership skills had been recognized by his election as an official of the Airline Pilots Association, and he'd given dedicated service to the Massachusetts Air National Guard. When he wasn't flying, Jim MacQuarrie spent most of his time working on his two-hundred-year-old Colonial home in New Hampshire and restoring vintage cars.

Second-in-command Ray Wagner coached soccer and swimming in his spare time and had two daughters, both Olympic-class divers. He too was a National Guardsman, flying helicopters and fighter jets in the New Jersey Guard.

Altogether there were sixteen crew on Flight 103. The flight attendants came from many backgrounds. One was Finnish, another Spanish. Elke Kuhne was West German. A passenger on one of her previous flights had been so impressed with her service that he'd written to Pan Am: "It is only a person of such high caliber as Elke Kuhne that makes the cost of flying worthwhile." A similar testimony had been received from another passenger for Filipino Lilibeth McAlolooy: "If one of your goals is striving for excellence among your employees, you've accomplished that goal in Lili. It is because of her that I will fly Pan Am in the future." Lili was engaged to a Pan Am employee in Frankfurt.

At Prestwick Air Traffic Control Center on the southwest coast of Scotland, things were beginning to quieten down after a busy day of transatlantic traffic heading through their sector because of the gales. At 6:58 P.M., as the flight attendants were beginning to serve drinks and hand out the earphones for the in-flight movie and entertainment channels, PA 103 made contact with the ground.

MacQuarrie had left his seat, leaving copilot Ray Wagner in command. Wagner told Prestwick of his intentions and current position. "Clipper 103 requesting oceanic clearance. Estimating fifty-nine north ten west . . . requesting flight level 310, mach decimal eighty-four."

In Prestwick's darkened control room, controller Tom Fraser cleared the flight, understanding Wagner's message as his course: an intended altitude of 31,000 feet and an airspeed of 540 miles an hour. As they flew on over the Scottish border, the crew of Flight 103 would have been doing everything they could to get the flight back on schedule and as close to the advertised local time landing time of eight-forty P.M. Tom Fraser called back to 103 at 7:02 P.M. "Clipper 103 is cleared from fifty-nine north ten west to Kennedy."

Elsewhere in Prestwick Control the plane's progress could be seen on radar, the boxed green dot of the jumbo moving slowly across the screen with each sweep. That slow progress was being watched routinely by controller

Alan Topp. The small green dot inside a box was just another flight on just another night.

Seconds after that clearance from Fraser, his colleague jumped as the picture suddenly changed. The single box had become five. He looked at the screen next to his, fed from a different system, but the picture was the same for a few seconds, and then there were no boxes at all. The controller shouted across to the shift supervisor, but he was busy handling a report of an explosion on the ground. At the Eskdalemuir Earthquake Monitoring Center of the British Geological Survey in Dumfriesshire, the normally straight line of the seismographs jumped at 7:03 P.M. They recorded an earth tremor of 1.9 on the Richter Scale.

Clipper *Maid of the Seas* was no more. The huge aircraft had been devastated by a massive explosion right under the cockpit, in the most sensitive area of the plane. The force of the blast and resulting depressurization caused it to break up into thousands of pieces, throwing its human cargo into the blackness of the night five miles above the ground, and falling—some alone, some in pairs, some still strapped in their seats, some shattered by the blast—downward to the Scottish countryside below.

As the bodies fell, the force of the air rushing past them ripped the clothes away from the limbs, and pieces of human anatomy were stripped of tissue by the friction. Most thudded into the ground in the fields stretching out from Lockerbie, the force of the impact making them sink inches into the ground softened by the heavy rain of the previous few days. In the space of a few seconds, 259 human beings going about their business or relaxing at the start of a long flight to New York had been turned into Britain's worst-ever air disaster, some blown apart, some mangled, and all dead in the darkness of a gale-swept Scottish winter evening. Fathers, mothers, sons, and daughters, whole families were wiped out in seconds and impacted into the face of the earth.

Sixteen-year-old Melina Hudson was flying home to Albany, New York, after first term at school in Exeter in the West Country. It had been arranged through an exchange program, and during that Christmas term, Melina had been a big hit with her classmates so far from home.

Mark Tobin, a student from Long Island, had been attending Syracuse University's overseas program in London. He and many of the party of thirty-five from that university had been sitting near each other in the center section of the jumbo. The term in London had given Mark Tobin the chance to have a look at the BBC, all useful in achieving his ambition to be a sports broadcaster. Sport was the mainstay of his twenty-one-year-old life. Ice hockey was his passion, although his participation had been temporarily shelved because his lawyer father, Joe, said the game was impinging too much on his college work.

Mark had worked hard to pay for the trip, taking two part-time jobs, one as a security guard at New York's fashionable Bergdorf Goodman department store, the other as a lifeguard at the swimming pool of the Ramada Inn near his parents' home in Hempstead, Long Island. He was planning to go back to the Ramada; instead, the hotel did the catering for his funeral.

Thirty-six-year-old Department of Justice lawyer Michael Bernstein was heading home to California, having scented success in his latest mission. He was attached to the Office of Special Investigations, which hunts down alleged Nazi war criminals who gave false information to enter the United States, and arranges for their deportation. He'd been in Vienna talking about the case of an Austrian national, a former guard at Auschwitz concentration camp, who had lied his way into the U.S. in 1952. The man had admitted his past to Bernstein and his colleagues, and they were now trying to get the Austrians to accept him after his deportation. Veteran Nazi hunter Simon Wiesenthal had been deeply impressed by Bernstein's skill and determination; he would personally have an "In Memoriam" tribute to the lawyer inserted in the *New York Times*. Months later, Bernstein's hopes were posthumously realized: a little-noticed press release from the Justice Department, dated 27 March 1989, stated that the Austrians had accepted the former guard and that his departure from the United States was imminent.

The approach of Christmas was the reason why many were on the flight that night. Clayton Flick and Claire Bacciochi had become engaged on November fifth and were to be married in 1989. They were flying to New York from their homes in the British Midlands for a post-engagement shopping trip. Now Clayton, twenty-five, and Claire, nineteen, lay dead on a Scottish hillside. It was the end of a personal dream that had started in the summer in a nightclub.

Paul Jeffreys, thirty-six, was a former guitarist with the pop group Cockney Rebel. He and his twenty-three-year-old bride, Rachel, were taking a belated honeymoon, three months late. Paul was working for a record company, having left Cockney Rebel when the band split up in 1977, two years after their famous hit, "Make Me Smile."

Another man well known in the pop world was on the flight: Bill Cadman, thirty-two, now working in London after having left his native Liverpool. He'd helped design the sound systems for the opening of the Tate Gallery at Liverpool's Albert Dock, but previously he'd worked with Pink Floyd.

A devout family of four from Surrey were flying to the U.S. to spend Christmas with relatives on the east coast. John and Geraldine Stevenson, thirty-eight and thirty-seven, from Esher, died with their daughters, Hannah, ten, and Rachael, eight.

The takeoff delay meant that Bernie McLaughlin was able to catch his flight to death. If it had taken off on time, the thirty-year-old computer sales director would not have been aboard. He had not left enough time for the journey to Heathrow from his home in Bristol.

Bernt Carlsson, a personal friend of Yasir Arafat, was the de facto United Nations–appointed governor of the fledgling state of Namibia, and had been working to prepare that territory for independence. U.N. Secretary General Perez de Cuellar was to say: "His death, just as the door to Namibia's independence was opening, was untimely in the extreme."

Nineteen-year-old Helga Mosey was returning to her job as a nanny in New Jersey, traveling from her Pentecostal minister father's home in Warley in the West Midlands. She was to have returned in September, to study music at Lancaster University.

Among the crew that night was Spanish-born Nieves Larracoechea. The thirty-nine-year-old had often said to her German-born, insurance-broker husband, Frank Rosencrantz, how worried she sometimes became about the legendary trouble of Pan Am's finances. She had never mentioned safety fears.

More than most others, Bill Leyrer, forty-six, described as a ship broker, would have paid attention to the security precautions surrounding his flight. He was a frequent traveler and was heading home to Bay Shore, New York, after one of his many trips abroad. Two years before, a quirk of fate had saved him from being involved in a hijacking. He had been booked on a Pan Am flight from Karachi but had to switch flights at the last minute. The plane that he had intended to take was stormed by hijackers who breached airport security by driving onto the tarmac disguised as officials. They opened fire on the passengers, killing seventeen and injuring many more.

Another quirk of fate cost chiropodist Ingrid Smith her life. Mrs. Smith, thirty-one, had been visiting her mother and father at their home in North Hykeham, Lincolnshire. She had planned to stay another day, but after learning that her Pan Am pilot husband, Bruce, was to be working over Christmas, she decided to go back early. Mrs. Hilda Ledgard says that her daughter went to Heathrow unsure whether she'd get on the flight. "The last we heard from Ingrid was when she phoned and said, 'Mum, I've got on.'" It was to be the first Christmas they were not able to be together. As Flight 103 crashed, Captain Bruce Smith was flying a planeload of passengers from Bermuda to New York.

Julian Benello was a brilliant twenty-five-year-old classics postgraduate at King's College, Cambridge. He'd decided at the last minute to spend Christmas in New York and, because of the light load on Flight 103, managed to get on board.

At about seven-twenty P.M. the phone rang on the desk of the Pan Am flight controller on duty at Heathrow Airport. It was air traffic control telling Brian Hedley of the disaster. He pressed the panic button. JFK was informed. Command posts were activated. In Scotland, Pan Am's operations manager at Prestwick Airport, Roddy Anderson, was given a police escort for his sixty-mile dash to Lockerbie. Strathclyde police set up a casualty bureau with special hotlines for relatives. That was duplicated at Heathrow.

At Heathrow, Pan Am executives requisitioned one of their 727's—ironically, the clipper *Surprise.* They had to restrict the number of passengers to sixty-five to allow it to land at Carlisle Airport. It carried staff from the Air Accident Investigation Branch and Aviation Minister Lord Brabazon, grandson of one of the great British aviation pioneers. Also on that flight were London-based men from the CIA. The plane arrived in Carlisle five hours after Flight 103 had disappeared from the radar screen, its landing at Carlisle made tricky by the gales and driving rain.

It was wet and windy as Helen Tobin struggled out of the grocery store with over $150 worth of groceries that were to be transformed into Christmas lunch at her home in Hempstead, Long Island.

There was one item that had eluded her so far—a bulb for an overhead light in her den. Staff in each of three stores had sent her on a search around other shops in the New York commuter suburb. The rain, driven by a gale, had ruined her new hairdo. The search for the bulb had almost ruined her temper. Finally Mrs. Tobin found what she had been looking for and got into her car for the short drive home.

She had not had time to listen to the radio, but now turned it on in her car during the drive home. Peering through the windshield wipers, the mother of seven was only half listening as she mentally went through her grocery list to make sure she had all that was needed.

The Tobins' son, Mark, had had his flight on Pan Am 103 confirmed far enough in advance to be able to send his mother the bottom part of his confirmation note with the flight time. Next to it he'd written one of his characteristically short notes: "No more phone calls."

When the news came on the radio and the flight number was given, Mrs. Tobin knew her son was dead.

It was a family habit for Mrs. Tobin to toot her car horn twice as she pulled into the drive of their home if she had groceries to unload. "Whoever's in the house has to come out and unpack the trunk of the car," she explains. This time, however, she forgot the custom, figuring that her family would be in the house eating and talking as she arrived. "I got in and said I've got to call Dad at the office," she says, unaware that the family already knew.

Brian, her son, said, "No, talk to Dad, he's in the living room."

"I knew if Dad was home, he knew," Mrs. Tobin says. "Those poor kids worked to empty the car and put everything away, but they didn't notice a packet of shrimp in the trunk. It was to be the special that weekend. We didn't find it until Christmas Day."

Later that night the phone rang again in the Tobin household. It was the police at Heathrow Airport telling them that Mark had apparently boarded the flight. The outlook was grim.

The telephone had been ringing all night with calls from Mark's friends from the university and elsewhere. A State Department official also called to give them a twenty-four-hour hotline number. But within twenty-four hours the hotline went unanswered.

Mrs. Tobin, a devout Catholic, was unable to sleep on that Thursday night (or on any night that week, for that matter), and got up at five A.M. to put her thoughts down on paper.

"I'd written three short essays related to Mark. I'd asked the children to write down their memories as well. I called the State Department hotline that morning, and there was no reply.

"At mass that morning the pastor gave a beautiful homily, talking of Advent, preparing for the arrival of a son and how hard it is now to face no homecoming at Christmas, no arrival of the son we were awaiting. He went on to say our consolation has to be reunion in the afterlife. And his final words people have quoted often since then: 'Jesus Christ lives, Mark Tobin lives. Praise God.' "

The Tobins are sharply critical of the way they were treated by Pan Am. In the hours after the crash each family of a passenger was assigned a Pan Am representative who was supposed to keep the family in touch with developments and answer any questions.

"A girl introduced herself to me on the phone," says Mrs. Tobin, "and said she was our representative."

Helen's husband, Joe, a lawyer and retired judge, interrupts: "We later learned she was a ticket salesperson, one of their better sales agents. We had great difficulty communicating with her. She admitted she was not up to it and tried to get off the job, and when she tried to get off the job, they gave her another family to contact.

"I eventually asked Pan Am to replace her, and we got a series of people who I talked to, and my recollection was there was one woman, but mainly men, all very cooperative, and seemed to be with it in terms of furnishing information we were looking for.

"This [first] woman said she was going to be 'our buddy.' It was an expression I had not heard since my days in Scout camp, when we had to have a buddy with us in the water. She was ill-equipped to handle what she was doing and she agreed she should not have the assignment."

Mr. and Mrs. Tobin are a quiet-spoken couple from the heart of middle-class America. They talk of their grief in measured, thoughtful words laden with emotion which turns to tears as words and phrases trigger memories of their son. Mr. Tobin has to fight back tears as he says

Mark was the undoubted favorite of his mother, the son around which the family revolved.

All through the night of December 21 phones were ringing in houses and apartments across the United States, though mainly in east-coast cities.

In Helen Engelhardt's apartment on Brooklyn's East Twenty-first Street, the telephone rang. "Is this Tony Hawkins' wife?" the voice asked tentatively.

"No, it's his widow," snapped back the reply. Helen Engelhardt knew. Her husband Tony had been in London on family business. He'd phoned the day before to ask if she minded him staying a little longer. "What's twenty-four hours?" she had said.

That phone call had been hard. What was to come was the hardest thing she'd ever done in her life.

Helen asked her six-year-old son Alan to sit next to her on the couch. "The plane Daddy was on has been in an accident."

"Was he hurt?"

"He's dead."

After a while Alan asked if that meant he was now all alone with his mother.

"No, you have your friends and family too."

Alan pressed his head deep into one of the cushions on the couch, then looked up and said, "Well, you can get married again."

In the weeks that followed, Helen was able to gain comfort from a bereavement group set up for the sixty or so families in the New York area that had lost relatives in the crash. But for now she was alone with her son. No one could, or can, feel what she felt.

Like any couple, she and Tony had had their ups and downs, but that autumn had been wonderful. Things were getting better. Tony Hawkins was a British citizen, a natural comedian well liked by their large circle of friends.

With the tragedy came the problems. He'd allowed his three life-insurance policies to lapse, but had been too embarrassed to tell his wife.

There was the coping day to day: "Tony used to wash the dishes. Now if I don't wash them, they don't get washed. Tony used to make Alan's lunch. Now if I don't make it, it doesn't get made."

For Alan there are the (on the face of it) inexplicable tears: "I'm upset because I can't find my sock."

That caller from the airline had asked Helen if she wanted to go to Lockerbie. Preparations were being made to take anyone who wanted to make the journey as quickly as possible. "There is no place in the universe I'd like to go to less," she had replied.

As the circumstances of each victim of the disaster were unique, so also were the responses of their relatives.

Tom Ammerman's brother Bert, the high school vice-principal from New Jersey, jumped into his car on hearing the news and headed to Kennedy Airport. Some had arrived before him, others drifted in later. Television crews also headed out to JFK that afternoon. They were rewarded with pictures of relatives of passengers on Flight 103 collapsing on the ground in uncontrollable grief—hysterical, unbelieving, and in shock.

Susan and Dan Cohen had fled their home at Long Island on seeing the news of the crash on television. They had been expecting their daughter, Theodora, twenty, home that night for Christmas. She too had been with the Syracuse contingent in London. As Dan Cohen drove along the Long Island Expressway, he twice had to stop his distraught wife from throwing herself out of the car and into the traffic.

The grief on the faces of Mr. and Mrs. Cohen and on those of the other relatives arriving at JFK was obvious to Pan Am officials who picked them out from the crowds in the airport and took them into a private room on the first floor.

Bert Ammerman arrived at JFK about eight o'clock. "The information was so chaotic, I decided the only place to be was at Kennedy. I met my sister-in-law and her father at the airport."

It was obvious to Ammerman, from the first TV coverage of the scene in Lockerbie that he'd watched before leaving for the airport, that his brother Tom was dead. He knew decisions were going to have to be made.

He knew he had to be with his sister-in-law to help her, and to find out for himself what had happened. Within minutes of his arrival, Ammerman found out. Pan Am officials confirmed his fears and said that there had been no survivors from the plane. He stayed with his sister-in-law at Kennedy for another three hours, waiting for verification from Scotland.

That came at about ten-thirty P.M., two hours after the plane should have landed. Pan Am people moved qui-

etly and slowly among the relatives, telling them individually that their loved ones were dead.

Ammerman says that, at this point, he and his sister-
in-law had asked if there was an opportunity to go to Scotland: "Pan Am said 'Absolutely,' and we said we wanted to
go out on the first flight."

The same offer was made to the rest of the hundred
or so relatives in the now-crowded lounge, but few were
insisting on traveling as quickly as the Ammermans.

The first flight that relatives were offered was to take
off at seven the next night, Thursday, December 22. It
was an overnight trip, and thirty-two relatives took advantage of it. They had slept little by the time the aircraft
arrived at Heathrow at eight-thirty on Friday morning.

Ammerman says he was tipped off that the airline
wanted their journey to end in London. "We were told,
thank goodness, by a Pan Am employee that they were
going to try and stop us in London and put us up in a hotel
for a few days. But the person said if we insisted, they
would fly us up to Lockerbie."

And that's just what Bert Ammerman did. When it
was suggested he stay in London, he asked why. It was,
said airline officials, to make sure people in Lockerbie were
ready for them. Seven insisted on going and were flown on
the shuttle up to Glasgow. "They tried to stop us again in
Glasgow, and we said, 'No way,' and they got a bus and
took us on a journey of about an hour. The bus stopped at
a school in the middle of nowhere, and I remember saying,
'How far are we from Lockerbie?' and they told me about
three minutes.

"I said, 'What the hell, we've traveled for twenty-four

hours, what is three minutes? We want to be in Lockerbie,' and they put us back on the bus and brought us over to the Academy."

When those first seven relatives reached Lockerbie Academy on Friday afternoon, December 23, their impression was one of total chaos. The imminent arrival of the first American relatives had given the press a diversion from the still unfolding stories of the disaster on the ground.

As the relatives walked from the bus into the Academy, the local secondary school that had been hurriedly pressed into service as police headquarters, they tried to ignore the questions being shouted from the nearby reporters. "It was just a circus," says Ammerman.

The twenty-five relatives that had decided to stay in London were put up by Pan Am at the Royal Garden Hotel in Kensington. There, officials from the U.S. Embassy and Pan Am executives gave regular briefings on what was happening in Lockerbie, all the time gently suggesting that a visit to the disaster town was not yet advisable.

Thirty-five-year-old management consultant Peter Dix had died above Lockerbie that night, a late booking on Flight 103. It was to be just an overnight visit to New York for a pre-Christmas business meeting. His wife, Elizabeth Delude Dix, did not know for sure if he was on the flight. She was not contacted by Pan Am—in fact, she still had not been officially told of her husband's death by Pan Am by the first week in February. The only way she was able to find out if Peter had been on the plane was to call a reporter friend in New York, who in turn phoned a friend at Pan Am who was able to discover, unofficially, that the Pan Am computer listed Peter Dix as having been given a boarding pass for Flight 103.

On Christmas Eve, Elizabeth Delude Dix found out about the briefings at the Royal Garden Hotel, and, uninvited, turned up to try and find out more. She was greatly angered by her treatment. First of all, she was told that if her husband's body were found, she should not see it until reconstruction work had been done. She told the official not to dare do that. "I just want Peter washed," she said.

Her brother-in-law, Ian Dix, says that sense of anger was shared by the American relatives at the hotel. They complained of not being able to receive or make telephone calls.

Eventually, says Mrs. Dix, they had all had enough. They sensed Pan Am was involved in a damage-limitation exercise, but the relatives decided that they were no longer going to be part of it. They insisted on going to Lockerbie, and on Christmas Day, Pan Am flew them to Glasgow, and then they were driven by bus to Lockerbie. The Dix family had, by this time, had enough of Pan Am, and instead of going by bus, hired a car at the Glasgow airport to allow them freedom of movement away from the shepherding of the airline.

Soon after arriving at Lockerbie, Mrs. Dix drove out to Tundergarth, where the cockpit was lying in the field. "I knew instinctively that Peter had been nearby, and I walked across the road to look over a wall at the nose cone. I was surrounded by policemen. I wasn't hysterical, I just wanted some space. It was like having police at your wedding or your child's christening. I was at the place where Peter had spent his last time on earth, and policemen kept taking my arm."

Peter's brother Ian Dix says he thinks the visit to Tundergarth was a PR exercise for the relatives who had arrived in front of them on the Pan Am bus. There were more police than relatives, "as though they were expecting a riot."

A social worker had driven down from Glasgow with the Dix family and, at Tundergarth, had agreed they all get out of the car. Ian Dix says he heard a policeman shout to the social worker, "You're in deep shit now," for allowing them out.

Elizabeth Dix's ordeal culminated in a near stand-up fight with an American embassy official. She had been trying, at the request of the police, to find out from Pan Am, from anyone, her husband's seat number. As well as being puzzled that the police did not already know this, Mrs. Dix was frustrated at the seeming reluctance of anyone to help. Pan Am even told her that that information was confidential. Next she tried the U.S. Embassy office in Lockerbie, where an official became very irritable. He lunged at her, saying: "Your relatives are in my office causing a ruckus." Someone moved between them—a stranger who rushed to comfort Mrs. Dix—and the row subsided.

3

DEALING WITH DISASTER

"It is impossible to even imagine such an
extraordinary tragedy."

As scores of police from all over Scotland arrived in Lockerbie, they were formed into search parties and sent out to scour the area around the town, trying to establish how far the wreckage and bodies from the flight were scattered. Most of the men arriving in the town that night had never been to Lockerbie before. They were going out into unknown countryside, in the dark, and in the rain.

All that could be done from the ground was to check the areas visible by flashlight from roadsides. It was up to the helicopter crews with their powerful searchlights to try and pick out the main areas of wreckage.

As each was pinpointed, ground searchers went out. There was always the hope that people might be found alive, but that was fading quickly as the search parties found more and more battered and broken bodies, some scattered and lying alone in dark and wet fields, others entwined in the twisted wreckage of the aircraft.

By midnight it became clear that there were six main areas of wreckage, stretching out from Sherwood Crescent roughly in a straight line northeast of the town. It appeared that the wings and connecting section of fuselage had crashed into Sherwood Crescent, and that the almost full load of aviation fuel for the three-thousand-mile journey to New York was the cause of the massive explosion that had illuminated the town. The continuation of the town's main street—Dumfries Road—was covered in rock and debris from the crater blown out of the ground by that explosion. Fire engines were parked on the right-hand side of the road, as seen from the town end.

The fires were out, but there was still a risk of new outbreaks and even the possibility of an explosion. Townsfolk picked their way carefully over the debris to see what had happened to the homes of their friends in Sherwood Crescent, but the road up to the neat little estate was barred by police.

Reporters, anxious to see firsthand the full impact of the crash site, stumbled their way across gardens burned and blackened by the explosion to view "the crater," which was about a hundred feet long and thirty feet deep. Tons of earth and rock that had formed the foundations of three homes had blown up into the sky and scattered around the town. The bigger boulders had crashed back down to earth on neighboring homes.

The whitewashed walls of the bungalows were scorched and blackened, and in the eerie flashing blue light of passing emergency vehicles, houses without roofs and greenhouses without glass could be picked out for a few fleeting seconds before darkness fell again. Everywhere was the stink of kerosene, the only real clue in Sherwood as to what had caused the destruction. Through the windows of some of the houses Christmas decorations could be seen, a grim reminder that the festive season was at its height.

As passersby were stopped by the press to tell their stories, many were too shocked to say anything. They could only shake their heads.

It was almost as though the explosion that had terrified the town had chosen its targets carefully. At the town end of the crater stood a house completely unscathed by the blast save for a blackening of the whitewash. Just a few feet away the three members of the Flannigan family and John and Rosaleen Somerville, their daughter Lyndsey Ann, aged ten, and their son Paul, thirteen, had perished. Only the body of ten-year-old Joanne Flannigan would be found. The rest had vaporized.

Reporter Andrew Lines was among those who dodged around the police cordon to see the terrible devastation of that night. "It was a sight that will live with me for the rest of my life," he says. Staggering over debris in the total darkness, he'd stood in what appeared to be a human stomach lying in a garden. Nearby, a woman's scalp hung from a hedge.

Other reporters managed to get up to Sherwood Park by walking through the forecourt of the Townfoot Filling Station—which had at first been thought to be the main crash site—past hanging electricity wires, over gardens and across rock-strewn Sherwood Park to the little crescent.

Northeast of Sherwood, over the railway tracks that bisect the town, the next deluge from above had landed. In Rosebank baggage had showered the long gardens that separate the two rows of council homes, pebble-dashed and painted dirty gray, which climb slowly up a slight hill to the top of the town. At one end of the trail through these gardens lay the ruins of Ella Ramsden's home, with a large section of fuselage visible among the rubble. A man who'd been walking up Rosebank just after seven, as the plane was crashing down, spoke of seeing that section twisting and turning in the sky, illuminated by the explosion. "It was as though it was looking for a safe place to land," he told neighbors. The gales were scattering papers everywhere around the gardens. Near the top, in Park Place, at the end of the rows of oblong homes, windows were shattered in the backs of the houses. Here a garden shed roof was blown away into the night. The power was off, so there was not even the lights from the houses to shine on the mess.

It took a long time for the residents and searchers to comprehend the scope of what happened that night. It was known that a jumbo jet, and not a military jet, had crashed, but people on the streets had no idea of the total disintegration of the aircraft and its cargo. Dark rumors were circulating of bodies piled up in various localities. The rumors would eventually be confirmed, but in the early hours of Thursday morning, few were prepared to believe them.

At one A.M. in the St. Mungo's Arms pub, the nearest of the town's watering holes to Sherwood, there were about half a dozen people sitting quietly in the bar watching television. The first television pictures of Lockerbie had been taken by news crews from Border Television just twenty or so miles down the road in Carlisle. They had enabled ITN to be first with the images that were to shock

Britain for days. The bulletin that hour started with pictures of houses on fire in Sherwood Park. In the Arms they were met with total silence as the faces stared intently at the screen high up in the corner of the bar.

One elderly man at the end appeared more moved than most. "His wife's missing," whispered the bartender to strangers in the pub. They were reporters. They began to ask the old man questions. Tears filled his eyes and he just shook his head and took another sip of his drink. Eventually he said in a quiet and shaking voice, "If she's all right, she'll ken where to find me"—a sentiment which took the strangers by surprise but was probably more rooted in shock than a lack of care.

There was no other news on the television that night. It was all Lockerbie. More graphic still were the pictures of relatives of the passengers arriving at JFK in New York and collapsing in hysterical anguish. It was a stark contrast to Lockerbie, where emotions are not worn on sleeves.

Farther out of the town lies the golf course, pressed into service that night as a helicopter landing pad. There, and at the next two crash sites—Halldykes and Balstock Farms, well out of Lockerbie and into the rolling countryside that surrounds the town—the bodies of passengers were mostly lying away from any plane wreckage, having presumably been sucked or blown out of the disintegrating aircraft. The farm dwellers had left their homes to see what the commotion was. Reporters hot on the trail of the wreckage found one farmer standing between two ambulance officers, all of them frozen to the spot. The expression on the farmer's weatherbeaten face said it all.

Questions were not needed, answers would not have been forthcoming.

In a dogleg deviation in the straight line of debris, the cockpit section of the plane had fallen in a grassy field just a few yards from Langholm Road. It was on its side, lying like some great fish head severed at the gills, its guts hanging out behind. The windows were shattered. Looking into the rear, the first people on the scene saw many of the crew, some still strapped into their seats, lying among the mess, their bodies horrifically mutilated by the metalwork of that section. As they flew overhead, helicopter crews could see MAID OF THE SEAS painted along the side in Pan Am's light blue lettering. As the yellow rescue choppers flew on, one horror after another was illuminated.

Just over the dry-stone wall at the edge of the field where the cockpit came to rest, stands the little parish church of Tundergarth. It was open that night—not for prayers, but to shelter searchers as they were briefed on their next task. On two sides of the church gravestones mark the final resting places of the people from the neighboring farms. Among them are obvious tragedies: the grave of a child who had died an untimely death in years gone past and saddened the community. No tragedy of a local nature could begin to approach that evinced by the carnage over the wall.

As police tried to come to grips with the situation, they were inundated with fresh reports, almost by the minute—new areas of wreckage, new problems to stretch an already overstretched and chaotic operation. They were besieged by the world's media, desperate for firsthand accounts. Phone lines were down and communication was near impossible. Teams were going out without radios; those who had sets found the airwaves jammed solid. Searchers were getting lost. Many had no real idea of what was expected of them, what they could do now, let alone what they were meant to be doing.

Senior officers had based themselves at the town's tiny police station, a single-story utility building where, in normal times, the biggest problems were if three people got drunk and disorderly on the same night.

As the ITN one A.M. news was going out, Dumfries & Galloway Chief Constable John Boyd was being told that an area of about ten square miles around the town had been affected by the crash.

Short (for a chief constable) and graying, Boyd was nearing the end of his career as a policeman. The reaction to dismiss him as a small town police chief would, in the main, be wrong. He does speak in the evidential phraseology beloved of Scottish police officers, but the job he was about to take up—Deputy to Her Majesty's Chief Inspector of Constabulary for Scotland—is an indication of the high regard in which he is held both by his colleagues and the Scottish Office.

No matter the size of the force, no region of Britain would have been able to take an event like Lockerbie in its stride. Like all other forces, the Dumfries & Galloway police had an emergency plan. But who would have planned for a jumbo jet falling on to an isolated town in the border country? Bigger forces would, no doubt, have been able to cope better, and one of Boyd's first actions was to turn to the larger neighboring regions of Lothian and Strathclyde to find help. This was forthcoming, but when it came, it was hard to deploy and hard to keep up to date with just what was happening and where.

Boyd admits that it was difficult to coordinate the assistance coming to Lockerbie. "As you will appreciate, with never before a disaster on this scale being experienced in this country, it was difficult to ensure we were maximizing these sort of resources.

"From the communications point of view, in the normal run of things we don't have thousands of radios. We have a sufficiency plus a reserve. But when one considers that by the early hours of the twenty-second we had almost eleven hundred police plus five to six hundred service personnel, plus other civilians, there's no way you can have sufficient radio systems for them all."

The scarcity of radios meant that, in many cases, if there were an important message to be relayed from the incident room in the police station, or from the field back to it, that message had to go by human carrier, and messengers got lost in the darkness and chaos countless times.

As the search effort wore on into the first hours of December 22, Boyd decided it was time to try and reach some sort of order in the operations. To this end a crisis meeting was convened in the police station at two A.M. with key personnel called back to headquarters to formulate a plan of attack.

As Boyd gathered his team around him, it was obvious that, no matter what the cause of the disaster, months of work lay ahead. They were embarking on an investigation of colossal proportions, and right now they could hardly account accurately for the searchers, let alone for whom and what they searched. Yet even though they did not have a single clue to go on, Boyd decided before the meeting that there was at least the possibility that the disaster would turn into a criminal investigation and he would therefore have to establish ground rules for an efficient investigation. Anything not done now might well be lost in the future if the crash were anything other than a tragic accident. In any event, there would have to be a thorough investigation of the wreckage so that aircraft experts could determine exactly what had happened.

It was the ground rules laid down at that first full meeting that would cause increased pain and anger to relatives of the dead. Boyd would agree with that view, but counter it by saying that it was those same ground rules that allowed his investigation to make the headway it has to date.

In the almost plodding (for the outsider) ways of the Scottish police, the rules were established. Accuracy was to be paramount; every single recordable detail was to be recorded, every position noted, no detail omitted.

Coordination was next. The flight carried many different classes of passenger, from honeymooners to vacationers, service personnel to key agents at the center of problems of world tension. Those on the flight—both passengers and crew—were also from all over the world, thirty-two nationalities in all:

American: 170	Dominican Republic: 1
British: 33	Finnish: 1
Indian: 6	Greek/American: 1
French: 5	Guyanese: 1

West German: 5	Iranian: 1
Hungarian: 4	Israeli: 1
Irish: 4	Jamaican: 1
Canadian: 3	Japanese: 1
Swedish: 3	Lebanese/American: 1
Argentinian: 2	Polish: 1
Filipino: 2	Romanian: 1
Italian: 2	South African: 1
Australian: 1	Spanish: 1
Belgian: 1	Sudanese: 1
British/Bolivian: 1	Swiss: 1
Czechoslovakian: 1	Trinidadian: 1

The "in-gathering" of evidence was also vital. Each key piece had to be corroborated to satisfy Scottish court procedures, which are laborious to the point of numbing the minds of any jury.

As that meeting broke up and senior officers left the police station with a clear idea of what was wanted, they still had little comprehension of what they actually had. The initial searches had confirmed suspicions that no one in the plane could have survived. Most of the rest of the night could only be used for checking and rechecking Sherwood to try and find any people still alive in the rubble of those homes and for refining plans for the morning. There were the homeless to help, the bereaved to counsel, and a welter of other human problems to contend with. There was plenty of everything that night, except sleep.

The next task for Boyd was the last of the four-point strategy he'd just outlined for his colleagues: the release of information to the media. It was now fast approaching three o'clock, and most newspapers were being printed and dispatched. There were still nearly a hundred reporters waiting in the nearby Masonic Hall, turned into a makeshift press center.

At 7:03 the night before, there had been just one journalist in Lockerbie—the local freelance who had found the destruction of large parts of his hometown so shocking and stupefying that he had been unable to file copy to the papers. Now the chief constable had to fight his way through the ranks of the press to reach the stage at the front of the small hall that had seen thousands of bingo nights and was now the central point for relaying news of a disaster that would have shocked the world at any time of the year, but was all the more poignant so close to Christmas.

As Boyd and other senior officers pushed through the throng, the television lights were turned on, cutting through the smoke of scores of cigarettes puffed on by reporters who had become increasingly restless as the waiting time for the news conference, originally put at just a few minutes, had stretched out to nearly two hours. With the usual paranoia of the press, the waiting journalists feared that, as they stood idle, their rivals were out getting stories.

The TV lights exaggerated the grayness of the chief constable's hair as he gave a brief outline of the disaster. "There can have been, I'm afraid, no survivors," he said. He gave the death toll from the aircraft as 276, a figure later revised downward by Pan Am staff in London, who had counted the crew in twice in their first calculations.

Those still with deadlines to meet hurried away to file

their copy and record pieces for morning TV and radio
bulletins. Others, whose work was done for the night,
went to get some sleep or a drink in one of the Lockerbie
pubs that stayed open for twenty-four hours that day.

By the time the news conference was over, a team of
specialists from the Air Accident Investigation Branch of
the Department of Transport were at the scene beginning
their work. Pan Am had already flown teams of their own
engineers to the scene. What was to become apparent was
that among their number were agents of the U.S. Central
Intelligence Agency, wearing the identification credentials
of the airline.

The relevant government ministers had also flown to
the scene: Scottish Secretary Malcolm Rifkind, whose department had responsibility for all sides of the emergency
operation that night, as well as Aviation Minister Lord
Brabazon. The United States Ambassador to Britain,
Charles H. Price III, had traveled with them to Prestwick,
and then by helicopter to Lockerbie. Rifkind held a news
conference and promised that all that could be done would
be done. He also refused to speculate on the possible cause
of the crash. Price told newsmen: "It is impossible, I think,
to even imagine such an extraordinary tragedy."

But as the night gave way to the cold December Scottish dawn, imagination was no longer needed, since the
painful and harrowing scenes were there for all to see.
Rescuers and rescued received the first impressions of
what had occurred in their midst. Parts of the town were
untouched. In a swathe stretching up the hill from Sherwood were the littered remains of personal possessions
and of human life itself. An engine lay in a hole fifteen feet

deep in the middle of a street at the north end of town. At Rosebank, a section of plane lay in the garden of Mrs. Ramsden's house. For those who cared to look more closely, it was obvious that many of the Syracuse University students had ended up in that garden, their young faces among the rubble, along with casual clothes and sneakers.

The houses at Rosebank had been built on land left over from Lockerbie's Victoria Jubilee Appeal, launched to raise cash to buy the now-defunct burgh council a real town hall. Now money was blowing around the gardens. "Strange sorts of money," said one of the residents, helpfully suggesting it may have been travelers' checks or bank drafts. Flight 103, apart from its passengers, also carried U.S. mail.

Up at Tundergarth Grange Farm, not far from the church and its new neighbor, the cockpit, Stewart Dodd, age fourteen, and his thirteen-year-old brother found over $500,000 worth of travelers' checks lying in one of their father's fields. They were large-denomination checks, tied together and torn in their descent from the sky.

Within hours of the crash the police and Scottish officials at the scene were told that the Prime Minister planned to visit Lockerbie first thing in the morning. The sight of Mrs. Thatcher, offering to the cameras her sympathies and assurances of speedy action, had become a set piece in any human tragedy on a large scale. A small team of police and civil servants had spent much of the night drawing up an itinerary for her, meeting with Downing Street.

The plans were to be thrown askew at the last min-

ute, when Buckingham Palace decided to send a member
of the Royal Family. The Palace is of the view that, since
the Royal Family is the embodiment of the nation, it is the
Queen and her family who must be the symbol of grief
and mourning for the nation in times of sorrow. This desire had been hampered by Mrs. Thatcher's quickness off
the mark, compared to the usual cumbersome arrangements that have to be made to take any given Royal away
from duties of the day, often fixed many months in advance. And protocol demands that a member of the Royal
Family cannot just turn up at the scene of a disaster.
There are Lord Lieutenants to organize, other arrangements to make, and formalities that have to be observed.

Lockerbie was to be no such case, however. At the
time of the crash, Prince Andrew, Duke of York, was just
an hour or so away on the other side of Scotland, where
his ship, HMS *Edinburgh,* was docked at Rosyth. In the
early hours of Thursday morning, he was telephoned by
the Queen's private secretary, Sir William Heseltine, and
told that he had been chosen to go to the scene of the
crash. When the Royal intention was made known to officials on the ground at Lockerbie, they hastily arranged
another VIP tour of the area, following the same route as
the one intended for Mrs. Thatcher but (coincidentally,
they say) timed to run ahead of her.

Andrew arrived in Lockerbie by car in the middle of
Thursday morning, wearing his uniform as a naval lieutenant. A press conference was promised, and a mob of reporters and cameramen assembled outside the police
station.

As the Prince's party pulled into Rosebank, police

hurried to the car and quietly told his advisors not to follow the route that had been planned. Minutes before his arrival more tangled bodies had been found in one of the areas he was due to visit, and the sight was deemed too unpleasant for the Prince.

Instead Prince Andrew saw Sherwood with its crater still smoldering from the night before and the smell of kerosene still heavy in the air. At Tundergarth he was obviously shocked. After a short briefing by the senior officer in charge of the sector on what had been found and what was going on, he was taken around the cockpit of the plane and, with some trepidation, took a couple of steps inside. There he paled as he saw the body of a flight attendant lying at his feet. Of all the scenes of mutilation around Lockerbie, few sights were as hideous as the inside of the cockpit, the bodies there having been battered beyond recognition. Officials believe that it was the shock of this scene that led the Prince a short time later to utter words that the people of Lockerbie will hold against him for many years to come.

After leaving Tundergarth the Royal party made another couple of stops before returning to the police station, where crush barriers had been erected to hold back the massed ranks of the press, many foreign, and many determined to push and shove their way to the front of the throng for a good shot. As the Royal car pulled up outside, Andrew turned to one of his advisors and asked: "What should I say?" He was briefed to offer his condolences and sympathy, keep it short, and get inside the police station. The press, needless to say, had different ideas, and after a short, sympathetic statement, Prince Andrew was sub-

jected to a barrage of questions and solicitations for views
and feelings that he did his best to answer. He then made,
in response to these questions, remarks that appeared un-
feeling in the extreme.

"Statistically, something like this has to happen at
some time on a town. It is most sad and unfortunate that it
happened to Lockerbie and so close to Christmas. It is
very sad for the town, but my deepest feelings and sympathy go out to the people, the families of those Americans
that died in the crash. I feel most strongly for those people."

With those words he earned the undying disdain of
many people of Lockerbie and, if subsequent press reports
are to be believed, the wrath of his mother.

As this was going on at the police station, Mrs.
Thatcher had arrived by helicopter at the golf course and
had begun her own, identical tour of the area.

She, some time later, told the same press mob: "It is
terrible for the people of this town and terrible for the
United States. They will be grief-stricken. We share their
grief. We also have grief here and we are doing everything
to help."

As the media attention at Lockerbie was focusing that
morning on the visiting personalities, the real and grim
work of the search crew was getting under way at the
various crash sites.

It was now known that 259 people were on board the
plane when it blew up in the skies above the town, but
there was still no clear indication of how many people on
the ground were dead. There were the people missing

from Sherwood and the people missing from the burned-out cars on the A74. Estimates of ground casualties were being revised down, but no one had any real idea what the final figure would be.

The first task was to try and recover the bodies lying scattered across the beautiful countryside around the town. It was obviously going to be a long task, and so priority was given to moving bodies that were in the public gaze, particularly those of child victims of the crash. It was realized that many of the bodies would have to be hunted out from the remote and inaccessible places where they had come to rest, and identification of them was going to be difficult. In some cases, it would be impossible. As Dr. Keith Little says, many of the bodies had simply disintegrated.

Policemen from all over central Scotland had been phoned at home overnight and told that they were going to Lockerbie in the morning. One man, whose phone was out of order, tells how a young uniformed officer knocked at his door shortly before five A.M. "I'm afraid I've got some bad news for you," he said as the bleary-eyed occupant opened the front door. Despite the fact that the older man was himself a policeman, his reaction to that opening statement was the same as most people's in similar circumstances: he felt his knees go weak, and a thousand ugly thoughts flashed through his mind.

"What is it?" he asked, fearing some unknown calamity.

"You're going to Lockerbie. I've got to wait for you and take you to the station," was the reply.

Relieved and angry, the pajama-clad policeman told

the younger man, "Don't ever do that to me again, you stupid bastard. I didn't know what had happened."

As this second wave of officers began arriving in Lockerbie, they were given a general briefing on what their duties were to be. Most were allocated to one of the six main crash sites, to begin searching.

One such officer was Detective Sergeant George White, who'd been bussed down the A74 from Glasgow that morning. In common with other CID men arriving in the town, he had been told to wear a normal business suit. His first impression of Lockerbie was that the town was not as badly damaged as the news reports of the night before had suggested. His second was that it was "bloody cold." It was a coldness that was to intensify, as the rest of the day was spent plodding around muddy fields in intermittent rain and in the biting cold wind that stayed near gale force.

Sergeant White was taken by personnel carrier up the hill past Rosebank and out of Lockerbie toward Tundergarth. On their way they passed a Salvation Army man who'd been detailed to stay with a body lying by the roadside. Communications had not improved much overnight, and the man had to maintain his lonely vigil while police drove back to the control room to arrange for the body to be removed.

One of the Tundergarth searchers tells of finding, in the field by the cockpit dead, an Indian woman and her two children, still strapped in their seats, sitting three abreast, their bodies apparently unscathed. In the same field was a youngish man sitting upright, naked save for his underpants. Lying next to him was an unbroken bottle of

Chivas Regal deluxe whiskey. "It was incredible," says the finder. "If you'd dropped it from waist height, it would almost certainly have broken. Here it was unmarked, having fallen virtually six miles. It just looked as though he was going to lean forward and pour himself a dram to warm up against the biting cold of the morning."

The newly arrived officers were given another briefing inside the church at Tundergarth. The cockpit had been examined. There were bodies stretching out behind it, there were bodies in the next field, and the next. "Each time we went over a hillock, seemingly at the end of the bodies, more were to be seen lying ahead. At first, there was one area we couldn't go into because of a large and none-too-friendly-looking bull. Eventually, someone found the farmer and the beast was moved."

During that first day in areas like Tundergarth, all that could be done was to try and assess proper procedure and establish priorities. As each body was found, a small brown label was attached to it and was given a number. Most of the men out scouring the hills that day found themselves in the area for the first time in their lives. Many strayed off into neighboring sectors. Some got lost.

Later that day one of the many subplots of the Lockerbie disaster began to unfold. Searchers were told that one of the reasons the plane had been late leaving Heathrow was that it was awaiting the arrival of four U.S. Air Force scientists. Detectives were told that, for security reasons, the pilot, Captain James MacQuarrie, had been given a package of vital documents in a sealed plastic folder to look after. One of the first priorities was to find the captain's body, which initial searches had established was not in the cockpit.

MacQuarrie's body was found that Thursday. It was one of the many scattered around the same field that contained the cockpit. There was no sign of the documents, so the search for them went on.

Some of the first people to arrive at the crash sites the night before had said that they thought they saw bodies moving. Again, on Thursday, some officers thought they saw similar things. It is clear from the doctors that everyone on board the plane would have been killed within seconds of its disintegration. Senior police officers say the movement must have been the wind knocking delicately poised bodies off balance.

"Many of the bodies that remained intact had no apparent injuries," says Sergeant White. "It depends how they landed. Some were pretty squashed, but it was remarkable how many of the bodies were still intact."

As they came to grips with death on such a massive scale, death that manifested itself by often gruesome injuries, the police had to try and turn their minds on automatic pilot. One man sums up the feelings of many: "Without wishing to seem callous, we were certainly aware that these were people we were dealing with, or at least they had been at one time, but we just had to get on with the job. I would not say we treated them as less than human, but there's like a wee switch you use to try not to think about it too much, or not at all."

The area around Tundergarth would eventually yield 160 bodies.

* * *

At the other end of the country, Transport Secretary Paul Channon went to the House of Commons on the morning of the last day's sitting before the Christmas recess. He made a statement on the disaster to the Members of Parliament, only a few of whom were in attendance that day.

The minister said that it was the worst air disaster in British history, and promised a full inquiry, with a report made public as quickly as possible. The two "black box" flight recorders from the clipper *Maid of the Seas* had been found, said Channon, and the Air Accident Investigation Branch was at the scene, being assisted by other government and U.S. agencies. The black boxes eventually revealed only an unidentifiable rumble, lasting only milliseconds, at the end of the tape.

There was a growing suspicion in Parliament, as well as at Lockerbie, that the cause of the disaster might well have been sabotage. A Member of Parliament, obviously with this in mind, asked if it would have been possible for a passenger to get on the plane in Frankfurt and get off at London with his baggage going on to New York. Clearly, said Channon, that would be the sort of area that would be looked into. There was no mention in his statement of any warnings about air security that may have been given before the disaster. Rather, he stressed that structural failure of the aircraft would be closely examined.

Not long after Mr. Channon had finished speaking in the Commons, news of such a warning broke from the U.S. Embassy in Moscow. The story was on the wires of the world's news agencies in time for lunchtime reports in Britain, and morning newscasts in the United States.

The agencies were reporting that staff at the Moscow embassy had been warned that an attempt to bomb a Pan Am flight to the U.S. from Frankfurt was to be made in the time prior to Christmas. The warning had been phoned anonymously to the U.S. Embassy in Helsinki by a man with a Middle Eastern accent. He had said that a Finnish woman would be duped into carrying a bomb onto the aircraft, and that international terrorist Abu Nidal was behind the plan. That warning, it transpired, had been circulated to all U.S. European embassies. In the staff canteen in the Moscow embassy, a notice had been pinned on the wall. It was a memo from a William C. Kelly, dated December 13.

> Post [embassy] has been notified by the Federal Aviation Administration that on December 5 an unidentified individual telephoned a U.S. diplomatic facility in Europe and stated that some time within the next two weeks there would be a bombing attempt against a Pan American aircraft flying from Frankfurt to the United States. In view of the lack of confirmation of this information, post leaves to the discretion of individual travelers any decisions on altering personal travel plans or changing to another American carrier. This does not absolve the traveler from flying an American carrier.

The last sentence refers to the fact that U.S. government employees are expected to fly American aircraft while on government business, and the carrier most often used is the U.S. flag airline, Pan Am.

Official reaction to the news of the warning was slow to come.

Mr. Channon was unable to answer further questions from Members of Parliament; he was on his way to the Caribbean island of Mustique for a Christmas vacation. Pausing only to confirm to the press that he knew about the warning of an attack on a Pan Am flight from Frankfurt, he flew off to the winter sunshine. The Foreign Office would make no comment.

At a White House briefing, President Reagan's press secretary, Marlin Fitzwater, was pressed on why government employees, but not the public, were made aware of the threat. He said that it was policy not to notify the public of all threats made against air routes because of the international damage that could result. Pressed again on why some people were told of the Helsinki threat but the general public were not, he shook his head and said: "I'm sorry I don't have any answers on that."

The State Department in Washington said details of the Helsinki warning had been passed to the British Embassy there. On December 22 a spokesman for the British Airports Authority, at Heathrow, said: "I can state categorically that no such warning was received."

At the time, Pan Am said that they too were unaware of any warning. That view was echoed by Pan Am security staff at Heathrow. A spokesman said: "Security checks were done for the lost flight in a perfectly normal manner. There was nothing exceptional about it, as far as our staff were concerned."

The International Air Transport Association, however, said that it was aware of the warning. It said such warnings occurred frequently but were always taken seriously.

By lunchtime on December 22 a group calling itself the "Guardians of the Islamic Revolution" phoned the Associated Press and claimed responsibility for the attack, saying: "We are undertaking this heroic execution in revenge for the shooting down of the Iran airplane a few months ago by the Americans and their keeping the Shah's family. We are very proud."

After the downing of the Iranian airbus over the Strait of Hormuz, which had caused Chris Papadopolous to prophesy about his adopted country's fate, Iranian leader Ayatollah Khomeini had called on Muslims the world over to attack U.S. targets.

In Parliament, Shadow Transport Secretary John Prescott accused his opposite number of misleading the House of Commons. Channon's junior minister, Michael Portillo, had admitted in a radio interview on Friday, December 23, that the government knew about the Helsinki warning, but said that it had been "confidential, classified U.S. intelligence information, and we didn't have the right to disclose it."

Prescott accused Channon of misleading the public as well as the House of Commons, and also said that he was guilty of gross insensitivity in flying out on vacation "as relatives of the dead were flying to Lockerbie to identify the dead."

Mr. Portillo wrote to Prescott:

When the Department received this bulletin [on Helsinki], we had it assessed and concluded that the enhanced security measures already in force in respect of U.S. airlines flights out of the U.K. were appropriate. Paul Channon was indeed aware of the existence of the warning before he went to the House to make a statement on the Lockerbie Disaster. He considered, as indeed you yourself said clearly, that "it would be better if we all withheld speculation about what may have caused the disintegration of the plane" until the investigation is complete. That is still his view and mine—a bomb explosion is only one of the possible explanations of the structural failure of the aircraft that occurred.

The line on taking all possible precautions was echoed across the Atlantic by President Reagan. When the warning was first revealed, he said: "If you stop to think about it, such a public statement with nothing but a telephone call to go on would literally have closed down all air traffic in the world."

The Helsinki warning was to be one of the greatest mysteries surrounding the downing of Flight 103. Undoubtedly, many U.S. government personnel might have been saved from a premature death by the notice pinned on the wall of the Moscow embassy canteen and those of other diplomatic facilities across Europe. What was to anger the U.S. and British relatives of the dead was that their loved ones did not have the same chance.

However, as police officers in Lockerbie continued their searches and identification tasks, it became clear that not all U.S. personnel had either known about or heeded the warning.

4

THE END OF A MISSION

"The day the CIA found what they were looking for . . ."

Among the hundreds of emergency workers piling into Lockerbie within hours of the crash were a number of agents of the U.S. Central Intelligence Agency. Their arrival did not surprise the senior police officers in command of the disaster area. It was an American flight, so it was to be expected that the elite of America's intelligence community should take an interest in the disaster. There could, after all, be a terrorist connection to what had just happened. The real reason for the CIA's arrival, however, was made known at only the highest level and in terms of absolute secrecy.

It is likely that Chief Constable John Boyd would have been told by intelligence men that some of their number had died in Flight 103 and that they were carrying with them documents of the highest level of secrecy classification. It was vital that these documents be found quickly, before they fell into the wrong hands. As the searches spread out from Lockerbie in the days after the crash, senior police officers in each sector were given confidential, and puzzling, orders. They were told to be on the lookout for particular items of luggage, but they were not given any idea of what that luggage might look like or what it contained. If they found it, they were told, they would know what they had found.

Six miles outside Lockerbie, past Tundergarth on the road to Langholm, farmer Chris Graham was taking stock of what had happened the night before. All night he and his family had done what they could to make sure that no survivors had landed on Carruthers Farm. When it was obvious that there were no survivors, they had tried to sleep. All the while, helicopters rattled back and forth overhead. Now, from his imposing farmhouse set among trees at the end of a short private road, he could see in the first light of Thursday, December 22, that substantial quantities of luggage and aircraft parts had come down on his fields. The lighter contents of the scores of suitcases that had burst open on impact the night before were blowing about. Clothing and other personal effects lay all around.

The farmer was particularly concerned about the many Christmas presents that had ended up in the creek that flows past the rear of his house. It saddened him to see the things that were to have been a child's delight on Christmas Day lying in the swollen water, some being swept downstream. He and his sons walked slowly along the banks, lifting the gifts out of the water and laying them gently down on the bank. Then an RAF helicopter landed just a few yards away and one of the crew ran over to interrupt the little rescue mission. The airman told the farmer to leave everything alone—he could be tampering with vital evidence. Displaying the independence of mind for which farmers in this often hostile countryside are famed, Graham left the airman in no doubt that he had no intention of stopping what he was doing. He would not like to think of children's presents being washed away. A compromise was reached. He undertook not to touch the bags of U.S. mail that had also landed at Carruthers Farm that night.

Graham's farm stretches from Langholm Road up to Torbeck Hill, part rough pasture, part trees, where sheep were grazing that morning. Graham remembers a lot of activity around his farm over the next few days, but the only thing that really stands out in his mind was the arrival, on Christmas Eve, he thinks, of a white helicopter.

An American came over from the helicopter and asked Graham not to go up on to Torbeck Hill that day—the only time he was asked to keep off part of his own land. He readily agreed, but joked with the stranger that he might have to stand up any ewes that were lying with their feet in the air.

That day the CIA had found what they had been looking for, or at least an important part of it. It was the remnants of a suitcase belonging to Charles Dennis McKee, an Army major involved in communications. McKee had spent his fortieth birthday immersed in a top-secret Middle East mission, the nature of which has never been officially revealed to Scottish police officers but which, from other documents found following the crash, can be seen to have been related to the continued holding of U.S. hostages in Beirut.

Having found part of their quarry, the CIA had no intention of following the exacting rules of evidence employed by the Scottish police. They took the suitcase and its contents into the chopper and flew with it to an unknown destination.

McKee was one of the Army's top military communications experts. He was based at Arlington Hall station, just across the Potomac from Washington, D.C., at the Intelligence Section Command. At the time of his death he was on secondment to the Defense Intelligence Agency, one of the hybrids of the American intelligence community. His role in the operation would likely have been to send back coded messages to Washington, and the suitcase's contents would have been sensitive: first, because of the messages that had been sent in both directions; and second, because of the codes used.

The determination of the CIA to recover the case and to ignore the "rules" of the investigation gave Scottish detectives a major problem. It was not until Major McKee's case was returned to the Academy police headquarters that the exact nature of the problem was determined.

Although it was December 28 before the police revealed that a bomb had brought down Flight 103, that theory had been worked on almost from the outset of the disaster. By Christmas Eve evidence to support it had been discovered and was being tested by explosives experts. Although there was still some doubt as to the exact nature of the explosive used, initial tests pointed to Semtex, the Czechoslovakian-made plastic explosive favored by terrorists the world over because it is both powerful and hard to detect in its predetonated form. McKee's battered and ripped brown imitation-leather suitcase bore marks of an explosion. It had obviously been close to the site of any bomb and, as such, was vital evidence.

McKee and the other CIA men had boarded Flight 103 at Frankfurt. The five-strong party were among the forty-nine passengers that transferred off the 727 to the *Maid of the Seas* for the second leg of the journey to Kennedy Airport. Their luggage was among those manhandled into the forward cargo hold of the jumbo jet, where police knew the bomb had gone off. For the Scottish detectives, that meant they had to investigate the possibility of the bomb being contained somewhere among the CIA men's luggage. Because of the nature of their operation and its location in war-torn Beirut, this was a strong possibility.

When I reported this line of inquiry on National Independent Radio, the police reaction to the obvious leak was swift and firm. Two officers arrived unannounced at my office in Edinburgh, demanding to know the source of my information. During an interview that stretched to four hours and was at all times professional and cordial, Detective Inspector Alex McLean said he had been ordered to discover the origin of the story and that he could not leave until he had done so. The fullest cooperation was given by me and my employers, Radio Forth, the Edinburgh independent station, but we were unable to help Inspector McLean with the main thrust of his inquiry. He, in turn, said that the Lockerbie Incident Control Centre viewed the story with such importance that if I felt that there was anyone in Britain to whom the sources of the story could be revealed, immediate arrangements would be made to facilitate a meeting. That, said the detective, included the Prime Minister, Margaret Thatcher.

Eventually a compromise was reached. I undertook to check back with my sources, but if they were not prepared to be revealed, that was as much as I could do. Inspector McLean said that if a revelation was not forthcoming, the police would take steps to have me precognosed, a Scottish legal mechanism by which a statement is taken by a sheriff from an individual under oath, and if answers are not given, imprisonment for contempt of court is a likely outcome.

The following morning the police at Lockerbie were told that, regrettably, I could give them no further assistance. It was again stressed that I had no information in my possession that could be unknown to the police. The position was resolved later that day when, in response to a parliamentary question tabled by the Scottish MP Tam Dalyell, Scotland's senior law officer, the Lord Advocate, said that no further action would be taken in the matter.

With McKee's case now in Lockerbie Academy, the chain of evidence had been broken. Scottish police officers had to repair the damage done by the CIA's disregard for the rules and secretly return the case to where it had been found.

Early on Christmas Day a small group of detectives were called into the Lockerbie Incident Room for a briefing from members of the investigation team and two CIA agents.

One of the investigation team briefed the small group at some length, but seemed to be evading the main point. Eventually one of the CIA men interrupted him to clarify what was planned for that day. McKee's case had to be returned to Carruthers Farm, to the exact position from which it had been taken, and that was to be combined with further detailed searches for pieces of expired explosive. Up on Torbeck Hill more pieces of Semtex were being picked up. After it has exploded, it becomes almost licoricelike and is relatively easy to identify.

The detectives split into two groups. The party with the case, directed by CIA men, did not make much headway. The mist had come down and it was hard to find their way around the hill—in fact, one of them got lost for a while. The detectives were still not entirely clear as to what was expected of them, but as they moved around the hill, it slowly dawned on them. They were, they thought, expected to "find" the empty case and sign statements and labels to that effect. They did not like it. They had little idea of what the case was or its importance, and they feared that they might find themselves at some future court hearing having to give evidence that was wrong and about circumstances they had no idea about. Finally the detectives called a halt to the operation and told the CIA men that they wouldn't do it.

Eventually McKee's case (presumably relocated by the CIA agents) was "found" by two British Transport police officers. In their ignorance, they were quite happy to sign statements about the case's discovery.*

This was not, however, the end of the CIA's delicate problems. There were other items that had to be found and returned safely—and unread—to Washington.

* The chief constable of the Dumfries and Galloway Constabulary has stated that, after thorough investigation, "no evidence whatsoever of anything improper has been revealed."

Agents, usually wearing badges that identified them as Pan Am engineering staff, remained on the ground.

Debris from the plane would eventually be found along a forty-mile corridor stretching roughly northeasterly from Lockerbie right across southern Scotland, over the border into England and up to the North Sea coast.

In northern Northumberland the corridor of debris cut through Kielder Forest, Europe's largest man-made woodland, and on to the bleak moors at Otterburn, used by the Army as firing ranges and training grounds. It was at Otterburn that the next vital piece of CIA documentation was found. Soldiers from Otterburn Camp had been drafted to conduct line searches of miles of moorland, picking up every single item that might be of interest to the investigators. Here soldiers found a sheaf of paperwork that gives the main clue to what the CIA were doing.

Along with McKee the five-member CIA team on Flight 103 had included Dan O'Connor, from Dorchester, Massachusetts, and Ron Lariviere, who lived in the heart of historic Alexandria, Virginia, outside Washington, D.C. They are officially described by the U.S. State Department as diplomatic security officers. They may well have been bodyguards in Beirut, but the Diplomatic Security Branch of the State Department is also widely used as cover for CIA agents. It also has an anti-terrorist and an anti-espionage role.

The fourth member of the CIA team was Matthew Gannon, from North Ardmore, California. He is described as the political officer of the U.S. Embassy in Beirut, but Washington sources place him as the Deputy Chief of Station of the CIA in that troubled city. Beirut has been one of the agency's unluckiest places. One of their top agents was kidnapped there and taken to Tehran where, it is thought, he was tortured to death as the Iranians tried to gain information from him.

Detectives also believe that there was a fifth member of the CIA team, a deep-cover agent who appeared to have no connection with the federal government. He was Bill Leyrer. That suggestion is laughed at by Leyrer's wife at her home in Bay Shore, New York. "If he was in the CIA," she says, "it's a secret he kept with those people in Virginia"—a reference to CIA headquarters at Langley. "Bill worked for the Universal Transportation Corporation in New York, and the World Food Program in Rome."

At the Universal Transportation Corporation in Manhattan, however, a spokesman (who declined to identify himself) said that Leyrer had simply rented office space from his company for about eighteen months. He had nothing to do with the UTC.

The presence of this particular CIA team on Flight 103 is one of the many ironies of the Lockerbie disaster. It is now believed by Western intelligence sources that the Lockerbie bombing was in direct retaliation for the downing of the Iranian airbus by the *Vincennes* on July 3, with the loss of 290 lives. If the CIA team had been involved in either negotiations with the people holding American hostages or had been planning a dramatic release attempt by force, they would have been dealing either directly or indirectly with many of the Iranian-backed terrorist groups that operate in Lebanon. The nine Americans in captivity in Beirut at the time of this writing are held by organizations that, in the main, can be connected to factions within the Iranian government—namely, the "Islamic Jihad, The Organization of the Oppressed," which also goes under the names of the "Islamic Jihad for the Liberation of Palestine," and the "Revolutionary Justice Organization." Scottish detectives believe that the more than $500,000 found by the farmer's sons near Lockerbie may have been part of a fund either to buy information or to pay a ransom for some of the hostages.

It seems clear from what was found on the ranges at Otterburn that the CIA men had managed to locate the exact position of at least two of the hostages. British Army searches discovered what appeared to be a detailed plan of a building in Beirut; two crosses on it are thought to mark the exact position of two hostages. There were also marks showing the positions of guards placed around the building, and under the plan was part of a narrative account of how a storming of the building might be achieved.

Elsewhere on the fields around Lockerbie was found another clue to the mission of the ill-fated CIA team. In an envelope that had been damaged on its descent to the ground was a Christmas card addressed to an individual at the U.S. Embassy in Nicosia, Cyprus, from where the agency men are thought to have been operating on the trips to Beirut. A strangely worded message on the card gave readers the impression that whatever it was that the CIA had been planning had been going to occur on March 11—which Scottish detectives assumed to be 1989.

When that day passed with no apparent developments in Beirut, Scottish detectives who had pieced together the story assumed that either something had gone wrong or the mission had died with its organizers.

5

THE INVESTIGATION BEGINS

"It's all about building, exclusion, and development."

Away from the "delicate" side of the operation, massive logistical problems were building for the police and other investigators. Space was to be one of the first. Chief Constable Boyd and his officers had to find room for what in the first few days after the crash could have been a figure of up to three hundred bodies, taking into account the people still undiscovered in the Sherwood homes and what officers still believed to be an unknown number of passing car drivers killed in the blast.

They were lucky to find a chemical warehouse in the town that was temporarily unused; the Dexstar plant became the central gathering point for all the property found by the searchers. The large floor space was divided along the lines of the growing areas of search, and property was put on the floor to correspond with the area in which it was found. There was a health hazard involved because of the contamination of property with blood, so biological protection suits were found for the officers examining what was brought in by the searchers. The Transport Department's Air Accident Investigation Branch based themselves at the Ministry of Defense establishment at Longtown in Cumbria, not far from the Carlisle airport. Here the wreckage of the jumbo jet was brought in and, while not exactly pieced together, gathered as far as possible along a grid plan of the plane. The devastation caused by the bomb and the descent to earth had shattered the plane into literally a million pieces. Apart from the cockpit section, the largest piece of the plane found to date measured just fifteen feet.

Police have always denied that any illegal drugs were found on passengers or in their luggage, but as one would expect on any transatlantic flight, people were carrying drugs. An area of the Dexstar factory was set aside for the secure keeping of these substances. There were three main finds. One of the students returning from the Syracuse University overseas school had a plastic bag containing "grass." The bag had ruptured and most of its contents had scattered to the wind, but still a handful was found and locked away. One of the American service personnel flying home for Christmas was found to have a block of cannabis weighing roughly two pounds strapped to his body. And, most significant of all, a substantial quantity of heroin was found in another suitcase. It is widely known that U.S. service personnel are sometimes used as drug couriers when they travel back home on leave because the chances of them being searched by security and customs at airports are held to be less than those of ordinary travelers.

The heroin find seemed particularly significant to police when they discovered it had been a bomb that had brought down Flight 103. The most foolproof way of getting a bomb onto an aircraft is to give it to a fanatical terrorist hell-bent on suicide to further his cause. Failing that, a dupe has to be found who would unwittingly take on the explosive—perhaps in the belief he is smuggling drugs.

Detectives at first thought that because of the total destruction of the plane, the charge of Semtex in the bomb must have been substantial. However, as pieces of expired explosive were picked up, along with the shattered remains of the radio cassette recorder into which the Semtex had been packed, it became clear that, in fact, the amount of plastic explosive used was quite small, perhaps just three hundred grams. The bomb had—by luck, officers believe—been placed in the forward cargo hold, right beside the jumbo jet's most vulnerable part, station 41, where the delicate electronics of the aircraft are housed. The explosive would have put them out of action immediately. The small hole in the fuselage caused by the blast would have grown within only tenths of seconds as depressurization and air friction ripped into the structure. Pieces would have come flying off—whole sheets of aluminum ripping away from the framework. Destruction would have been quick, complete, and terrible.

Since the outset of the inquiry, there have been two investigations running parallel to each other. Sources in Washington, D.C., say that within seventy-two hours of Flight 103 crashing on Lockerbie, the intelligence side of the inquiry had established why the attack had been carried out, on behalf of whom, and by which terrorist organization. The second investigation—that taking place on the ground, starting at Lockerbie but gradually spreading out over the weeks that followed—was the classic criminal investigation based on tried and trusted methods of detection: to establish the crime, the motive, the method, and the culprits. The Scottish police have won widespread acclaim for their painstaking search of some of the most difficult countryside in Great Britain.

As police were pursuing their classic criminal investigation, they were helped by a substantial quantity of high-quality reports from international intelligence-gathering organizations that had been tracking the movements of various terrorist organizations in Europe, particularly in West Germany. Much of this intelligence information had already been handed to the Federal Aviation Administration in Washington, D.C., for use in "security bulletins," which are routinely sent to airlines to help them gauge what level of security is required around their international operations. The intelligence that was helping police in the early days of their investigation into the Lockerbie disaster was to become a mine field for the politicians coming under attack from the relatives of those killed in Flight 103. As it became clear that this high-quality intelligence had formed the basis of substantial air warnings, the relatives became increasingly angry that little appeared to have been done by the airlines to tighten security.

For example, in the early days of the investigation, Detective Chief Superintendent John Orr, joint head of the Criminal Investigation Department in the neighboring Strathclyde region and now senior investigating officer at Lockerbie (and Chief Constable Boyd's subordinate), was made aware of certain events that had happened in West Germany two months before the Lockerbie disaster.

Acting on information supplied to them by the CIA, the BKA—the West German security police—had raided a number of houses and flats occupied by suspected supporters of the Palestinian breakaway terror group, the Popular Front for the Liberation of Palestine–General Command. Most important of all, the raids yielded a radio cassette recorder that had been converted into an obvious triggering device for an aircraft bomb. This, coupled with Detective Chief Superintendent Orr's later assertion that the balance of probability lay with the bomb being loaded onto Flight 103 at Frankfurt, meant that the finger of accusation was pointing strongly at the PFLP-GC.

Here is one of the many anomalies of the Flight 103 story. Mr. Orr and his ultimate superior, Scotland's senior law officer, Lord Advocate Peter Fraser (the equivalent of the U.S. Attorney General), have in their few public statements on the criminal inquiry been at pains to stress two things: first, that substantial and significant progress is being made; and second, that international cooperation with all concerned agencies could not be better.

Yet despite this alleged international cooperation, the West German authorities have been quick to deflect allegations of shortcomings on their own territory. As late as the end of March 1989, West German public prosecutor Jochem Schroeder was saying publicly that there was no evidence to suggest the bomb was placed aboard Flight 103 in Frankfurt. Privately, his office was also briefing journalists that the 26 October 1988 raid that uncovered the radio cassette device was totally unconnected with the tragedy.

It is, however, clear to officers close to the Lockerbie inquiry that, even from the earliest days of the investigation, certain and definite lines of inquiry were being pursued. It was almost as though those in charge knew what they were looking for.

The finding of the weapon is an important part of any murder investigation, and the fact that police were now investigating more than 250 murders made no difference. It is a testament to the ground rules laid down by Chief Constable Boyd at the meeting in the early hours of December 22 that the investigation has reached the stage it is at today. It takes an intimate knowledge of the countryside over which the wreckage of the plane and bodies were found to realize fully the difficulties faced by police officers and other searchers in the task. The actual luggage container in which the bomb and other Frankfurt luggage were held was blown to pieces and scattered over a forty-mile trail through woods, bogs, hills, and lochs. That container has now been largely reconstructed and a huge number of fragments of the explosive device found— enough to enable detectives, with the aid of forensic scientists, to conclude that it was a Toshiba radio cassette recorder, although a different model to the one discovered in Frankfurt.

Investigators were saved from the task of reconstructing all the luggage containers because it was obvious from the pattern of the plane's destruction that the main thrust of the blast had been toward the front of the aircraft, where the Frankfurt luggage container was located. An-

other reason for checking other containers—that is, those
originating in London—is that initial intelligence reports
pointed the finger of suspicion at West Germany.

Mr. Orr says: "It's fair to say that we know that, in an
aircraft of that size, there are cargo containers and a number of luggage containers, some of aluminum and some
fiberglass. We know the position of each of the containers
because of a certain system of ingestion into the aircraft,
and which contained what in general terms.

"Each of these containers has a unique number and
unique identification. Some, if not the majority, of the containers did not suffer damage consistent with an explosion.

"This is where the Air Accident Investigation Branch,
and other agencies that I am not prepared to talk about,
are adept at the identification of certain pieces of material."

Every single piece of "evidence" recovered during
those massive searches of 945 square miles of countryside
is individually recorded, and if need be, individual officers
can be found who could give evidence. What happened to
each item subsequently is individually chronicled.

The route the investigation took was to identify the
container that held the bomb, then the luggage that was in
the container, then the luggage that held the actual explosives. This was an extremely difficult task, considering the
force of the blast and the disintegration of much that was
around it. To underline this is the fact that the ten victims
from the plane whose bodies were never recovered were
those in seats immediately above the bomb. Their bodies
were completely destroyed by the blast and by the exploding fuel in the wings on either side.

"It's all a jigsaw," says Mr. Orr, "but the important thing about it is the strict professional approach which has been adhered to right from the start . . . no one can go in or exit from a crime scene without leaving something. That applies, albeit on a macro scale, in this type of scenario. It's all about building, exclusion, development."

Chief Constable Boyd sums up the balance between investigation and intelligence: "Any intelligence that may be made available in terms of security aspects of different countries involved has to be corroborated by hard, evidential facts, and we don't speculate. If you want to speculate, it is like permutations on a football pool."

Boyd stresses that they are fully aware of all the international ramifications— "We'd be stupid if we weren't"— but that they have still to attempt to find out who was responsible for the murder of all those people. "We are doing it in an international sphere, but we are doing it on the same principles as we would if one person was killed. Our horizons are very much wider. Don't think that we are being parochial in any way. We're not. We're taking all the advice and all the assistance of any aspect of expertise or intelligence that is available to us, but at the end of the day . . . we have to do it in an operational investigation."

Mr. Orr goes further. "We will go along with this as we have done from kickoff. It is the acquisition of evidence, backed up by statements and all the armory of investigation. This is no different from, dare I say it, an ordinary murder inquiry. After all, I've investigated hundreds of them. The important thing about this is that it is a macro scale, an international inquiry. Without letting secrets out of the bag, we have had tremendous assistance

from all the agencies who are working with us. There's a
pooling of information, with computer links to Germany
and Washington and London."

Mr. Orr says that the aviation warnings in circulation
before the bombing cannot be part of his investigation. "A
detective, being the animal that he is, investigates a crime.
Okay, you take cognizance of the warnings, and these are
peripheral aspects of the investigation, but it is not up to
me, nor is it part of my inquiry, to comment on whether or
not certain warnings had an effect.

"Clearly a crime happened and, as a result of the
crime, people were murdered. The whole principle is
about getting to the core. Who did it, why did it happen,
and, principally, to report in a totally objective way the
facts."

The simple term "gathering of evidence" cannot begin to
convey the true reality of what was facing officers on the
ground as the lengthy process of finding and recovering as
many of the bodies as possible went on. Day in and day
out the searchers found themselves at the forefront of
human endurance by the sights that they uncovered and
the work they had to carry out.

One officer involved in recovery says that he could
not look at the bodies he was dealing with. "Often they
were horribly mangled and all you could do as they were
lifted into a body sack was focus on the part of the body
you were holding, the least damaged part, and, when clos-
ing the bag, focus only on the zipper. I often felt like
walking away, but because there were a number of men
with me, I had to keep at it or they would have walked

away as well. When you were with others, there was a certain amount of bravado. It was when I was on my own that it really hit. Having said that, some men did walk away, and no one could blame them for that. Some men are still deeply affected by what they were doing in the days after the crash."

To help counter possible long-term psychological problems for the searchers, leaflets were regularly distributed advising of danger signs for men to look out for.

Dumfries & Galloway social-work director Tom McMenamay had been on the scene at Lockerbie since the night of the crash. He deployed a large portion of his department's social workers, along with other people from Social Services departments in Glasgow, and even some from Aberdeen, who'd dealt with the aftermath of the Piper Alpha disaster, an oil-rig explosion in the North Sea, east of Scotland, which killed 167 men on July 6, 1988.

McMenamay says that about 150 people from the town itself had help from social workers. In the majority of cases this was not formal assistance, but often simply providing someone to talk to, someone to share their horrific experiences with. A much smaller number of people required more formal help, and some are still being looked after by social workers many months after the crash.

In the end, no great numbers of emergency workers sought professional help from social workers to overcome their problems. Some in retrospect think they perhaps should have. Another experienced officer feels that when he was having to deal with his own emotions, he had no one to talk to about it. "You felt you couldn't come home at night and start telling the wife about what we'd been doing. Apart from the fact it was Christmas, you really just didn't want to burden them with what you were carrying."

It was mainly in the company of other officers that emotions, if not allowed out altogether, were certainly eased by conversation and drink. What was nicknamed the "stress factor" became an important part of the daily routine.

Many officers in the search parties were bussed to and from Lockerbie. The buses could be seen stopping discreetly near off-licenses where bottles of the "stress factor"—whisky and vodka—were taken on board. "Have another stress factor" was an often heard invitation as coaches sped up the A74 to home and a hot bath, sleep, and yet another early morning call, followed by the pre-dawn run back to Lockerbie for more duties.

McMenamay says he considered setting up a unit in his own department for staff affected by stress, but decided against it and instead asked the local health board to help any council staff in need of counseling. He made a conscious decision to allow this to be an entirely personal matter, and has made no attempt to discover how much this facility was drawn on, although it will, in terms of numbers, come out in debriefings.

Some police officers who thought they had been unscathed by the experience found this not to be the case. One discovered this driving on the highway that goes past the airport on his way to his home outside Glasgow. "It was dark, and I became aware of a plane coming in to land. Usually I'd have paid no attention to it, but my eyes became fixed on it and I was convinced it was going to crash. I remember saying to myself not to be so bloody stupid, but I started shaking and sweating and couldn't concentrate on the road."

Eventually he snapped out of it. The experience has not occurred again to this particular officer, but he supposes that many more of his colleagues must have had similar experiences, even if they did not want to share them with others.

In the first hours after the crash, the Victorian town hall at Lockerbie had been pressed into service as a mortuary. Soon the overspill of corpses went to the town's ice rink. Each body was accompanied to the mortuary by CID officers from the spot where it had been found. At the ice rink a team of pathologists, led by Edinburgh University's Tony Busuttil, carried out postmortems. Identification of the dead was often a difficult task, with families of those on the passenger list often being asked to supply dental records and fingerprints. Every effort was made to ensure that bodies did not get mixed up. Even with these precautions, two American families were sent the wrong ones, but the mistake was rectified.

It was a week before the American relatives were able to start taking home their dead. At twelve minutes past eight in the evening on Wednesday, December 28, the first five identified victims began their final journey home. The approaching noise of police motorcycles escorting an unmarked white truck broke the dark silence of the Lockerbie town center as the short convoy drew into the sight of about 120 residents, civic heads and emergency workers who had gathered by the town hall. As the truck carrying

the coffins of five people passed the crowd, Deputy Chief
Constable Paul Newall saluted.

Inside were the coffins of two children, Suruchi Rattan, age three, and his two-year-old brother Anmol. Alone,
they were completing the journey home to Michigan that
they had started a week before with their twenty-nine-
year-old mother, Garima. Her body had yet to be identified.

The first mix-up with bodies was spotted by Robert
Hunt, from Rochester, New York, who felt uneasy about a
description of his daughter Karen's personal effects.

He had the body returned to him and examined, and
was told it was not that of his daughter. A thorough investigation was ordered at Lockerbie and, because of the detailed accounts kept of each recovered body, police were
able to establish that a mortuary attendant had attached
the wrong labels to two coffins. Karen Hunt's body had
been sent to Massachusetts; the body Mr. Hunt had was
that of Mary Johnson, also from that state. That error was
rectified to the satisfaction of both families. However, as
we shall see, the next mistake with bodies was to be impossible to rectify and had to be hushed up.

6

THE PRESS

"They smelt as though they had spent the night in the
Bluebell Hotel."

In human terms, the tragedy of Lockerbie became personi-
fied in the form of fourteen-year-old Stephen Flannigan.
This bright and well-liked son of the small town lost his
mother and father, Kath and Tom, and his ten-year-old
sister Joanne in the crash. Their home disappeared in the
fireball of the wings crashing to earth in Sherwood Crescent with their nearly full load of aviation fuel.

On the night of the crash it was apparent to Stephen
that his family were lost. He spent the night with his father's oldtime pal, Bill Harley, owner of Caledonian Mo-
tors, tucked away behind the shops next to Lockerbie's
town hall. At the same time as Chief Constable Boyd was
chairing his first disaster meeting, Stephen was going to
bed across town. He says that as he lay in the flat above
Bill's garage, his mind was running wild. He was breathing
through his mouth, and his heart beat so quickly that his
breath was coming in shudders. Although such was the
chaos of the scene that it would be a week before a social
worker arrived to tell Stephen officially that his mother,
father, and sister were dead, he knew in his heart from
those first few hours that that was the case.

Overnight, a huge number of reporters and television crews had descended on the town. For them, Stephen's loss and the fact that he was now an orphan made a "good story," and one the popular papers especially wanted to have. Stephen's plight was well known to journalists by the time Prince Andrew was making his tour of the devastation. Bill Harley, already mourning the loss of good friends, was to endure something almost worse at the hands of the press.

"On the Thursday morning, I checked all my buildings to make sure there was no damage, which there wasn't, but there were pieces of debris lying about. I wanted to make sure that there were no bodies around before my staff started and the family came out.

"I opened up at eight o'clock and the press were in behind me, and it was a continual entourage from then on. Three reporters followed me into the showroom. They smelt as though they had spent the night in the Bluebell Hotel. Fortunately, for about three days nobody had a photograph of Stephen. We told the press originally that Stephen was in Dumfries, then they found my daughter's house and went to see if he was there.

"It's hard to remember exactly, but we were getting well over a dozen inquiries a day from the press at the garage and many more on the phone. It took them about a week to realize we lived up the stairs here. The inquiries were reasonably pleasant, but so persistent. Then, by the second or third day, it got to the point they were beginning to offer money for exclusive interviews with Stephen. They were saying things like, 'How would you like to take him on a holiday to help him get over this? Take him here, take him there.' "

Bill Harley says that all he wanted was to be left in peace to allow his family and Stephen to get on with a difficult situation. Eventually, however, he concluded that they would have to say something to someone. Stephen's uncle is a chief inspector at New Scotland Yard, and through him, Harley arranged an interview with the *Daily Mail*, thinking that once the story was published, the hunt for Stephen would die down.

"We went to the *Daily Mail* because their approach was the most professional and sensitive of the lot." The *Mail* had written Bill Harley a letter inviting him to get in touch if he felt an interview would ease Stephen's burden. "It was a nice letter."

That paper's reporter, Lynda Lee Potter, interviewed Stephen in Bill Harley's flat, and the paper published a center-page spread on January 2 that contained the most moving words written about the entire disaster.

"In other papers," says Bill Harley, "we were amazed at the quotes and stories that were fabricated from my wife and I. I think most of them were made up in the Black Bull and the Bluebell, to be honest." He says that the worst part of it was the persistence of the approaches. He'd just get calmed down after one confrontation when there would be another. To make matters worse, the *Daily Mail* interview did not have the desired effect. "It upset the Scottish papers. A couple of Scottish papers were a little more overpersistent for a couple of days afterward."

Then, in early January, it was discovered that Stephen had a brother, David, who'd left home after a family row and was living in Blackpool. That restarted the pressure on the remaining members of the Flannigan Family. "The *Daily Record* drove down from Glasgow and sat outside his flat in Blackpool until they got him. They did the same with Stephen's granny and grandpa." There was another group of reporters, from an unknown paper, that went to the house of one of Bill Harley's friends pretending to be social workers. They were spotted and thrown out. It got to the point that Mr. Harley became frightened to go up to people in his car showroom for fear they were reporters.

By way of compensation, the honesty and bravery of Stephen's interview in the *Daily Mail* produced a flood of letters from all over Britain giving him encouragement and support. Stephen told Lynda Lee Potter:

> "I feel my mum and dad are watching over me. Every night mum would come up to give me a kiss and say good night. When I'm on my own at Bill and Kate's [Harley] I look back on the happy times, on holidays.
>
> "I say my prayers night. I just ask God to keep my mum, dad, and Joanne well, to look after them. There's nothing else that can be done.
>
> "I liked my dad a lot. Bill has said to me that Dad and I were mates, not like father and son. Dad always made me laugh.
>
> "Bill has said now he expects to bring me up. He said there will be times when he and I are going to fall out, but that does not matter.

"I just want to make Bill and Kate as proud of me as Mum and Dad were.

"I feel a different person to the one I was two weeks ago. I've got a different family, a new family. I've lost my old one."

The media shock experienced by Bill Harley was being repeated over and over in the town where, on Thursday morning, twelve hours after the crash, the early morning businesses—the news agents, the bakers, and the two small cafés—were bathed in the bright lights of the television cameras.

It was hard for the townsfolk to walk up the street without encountering television reporters talking to cameras, taking the story of Lockerbie around the world.

"How are you, Ella?" someone inquired of Mrs. Ramsden as she walked briskly up the street.

"Fine, thanks," came the reply, "but I can't stop. I have to do an interview with CBS in a couple of minutes." Mrs. Ramsden casually rolled off the name of the American television network of which she would probably not have even heard the night before.

Many of the shops opened as usual that morning, partly to give a show of normality in a far-from-normal situation, and partly to service the huge number of people from all sectors drawn to the town by the disaster. In the shops the people of the town, who in the main all know each other, stood around and shared their experiences. The talking stopped only when strangers came in.

There was a weariness in the voices of some as they recounted for the umpteenth time to yet another newspaper, yet another reporter, the events of the night before. It was a weariness that would grow, in many, to become outright hostility toward the press. Not because of the media's insensitivity or sensationalism; simply because people were fed up with telling their stories over and over again.

There was further anger among both the townsfolk and the emergency services, generated by the large number of people who came to rubberneck at Lockerbie's disaster.

The impact of the wings and the explosion of the aviation fuel had sent a shockwave out from the crater, the force of which had actually buckled part of the A74 road. Past Lockerbie the four-lane highway was reduced to one lane each running north and south, and on both sides of the town long traffic jams built up, with people slowing down to get a good look at Sherwood. The cumulative effect was delays of up to one hour on the road.

Maureen Scott, who runs ballet classes in Lockerbie from her house in Annandale Terrace, tells of how annoyed she became watching passing drivers craning their necks for a better view as they passed. There were many small accidents on that section of road.

There was also a fear that children out at play would come across some grisly finds. Mrs. Scott's nine-year-old son Robbie used to play in the field that lies between Annandale Terrace and Sherwood. This was where Dr. Keith Little found the many hundreds of pieces of human bodies blown apart by the bomb and then the fuel blast. Robbie Scott and his friends have never gone back into that field.

* * *

What Chief Constable Boyd calls the "macro scale" of the disaster left macro logistical problems to be solved. For instance, the hundreds of searchers needed food and water. First the Women's Royal Voluntary Service and then the regional-school meals service ran a canteen at Lockerbie Academy that was open twenty-four hours a day and eventually served thousands of meals. A central-school meals service, though, was little help to those out on the hills battling against the biting cold to search out clues to the disaster. In the main, these people were kept going by Salvation Army mobile canteens that spent the days touring the main search areas and dispensing hot drinks and what hot food they could.

It was a Salvation Army captain who provided a near-comic footnote to one of the most horrific of all the recovery episodes.

A police searcher at Tundergarth, a sixty-mile sector that would eventually yield 160 bodies, had seen a hand sticking out of a puddle in a particularly boggy area of ground. He had gone as far up to it as he could without actually sinking into the mire, and was dumbstruck to see a woman's face staring out at him from the bottom of a peaty pool. More police and a squad of soldiers from the Royal Fusiliers were called in to examine the bog. They found that ten bodies had fallen on it and had sunk below the surface. As the six young Fusiliers, led by a sergeant, dug into the bog, it became apparent that at least one of the bodies had burst open on hitting a stone, and the mess it had made in the mire caused one of the young soldiers to vomit, which set off a chain reaction among the diggers.

Then the police noticed on a not-too-distant hill an American TV crew focusing their camera on the pale-faced group. They were ordered away.

There was a feeling among those at the sharp end that, when a grisly task had to be undertaken, it was best to press on as best they could because once stopped, it could be near impossible to go back to the work. That happened here, and because of the intervention of the Salvation Army. The Salvation Army man told the searchers to break for a while and have some tea. This, of course, outraged their sergeant, who saw his authority usurped. He ordered them back, and after a couple more minutes, just enough to satisfy discipline, the sergeant ordered them to down tools for a tea break.

On Christmas Eve in Lockerbie there was little of the festive season to be seen in the streets. Many residents had decided to press ahead with celebrations, but they were, in the main, parents of children too young to appreciate what was going on around them. Turkeys were still being stuffed, shop windows still wished their customers "Happy Christmas," but there could be little sincerity or anticipation in the felicitations.

Reverend Jim Annand had to prepare for his Watchnight Service. This year, instead of worrying about flowers, he had to contend with the media who wanted to turn into a world event what should have been just another service. He decided to go ahead more or less as planned, although he dropped the hymn "Love Came Down at Christmas" from the planned service.

The Christmas Day news bulletins around the world

carried pictures of that service—the church full to capacity, the congregation swollen by emergency workers who, because of what they were going through, probably had more need of God on that night than on any other in their lives.

On Christmas Day itself the morning service at Dryfesdale Parish Church saw the pews only half full. Reverend Annand told the somber congregation: "Shock and disbelief have so numbed our minds that only now are we beginning to comprehend what has happened to our community. Never before have so many people been killed at one time. Never before have so many innocent air passengers died at one time in our country. But we should never allow the magnitude of the disaster to let us forget that a disaster is made up of many small personal tragedies, all happening at the same time."

At the town's Roman Catholic church—where the parish priest, Father Patrick Keegan, was feeling the full force of the grief, having lost members of his congregation who had been real friends—the Bishop of Galloway, the Right Rev. Maurice Taylor, asked: "What meaning does Christmas have this year for the people of Lockerbie? What meaning does the air disaster have for the people of this town, which has now become a household name throughout the world?

"Father, if you are God of Love, why did you let this happen? Why did you allow the destruction of hundreds of innocent lives? Those who were citizens of Lockerbie? The many who had never heard of Lockerbie, but whose lives ended tragically in the streets and fields of this part of Scotland?

"And why do you permit so many people to have to suffer the cruel, tragic burden of bereavement? The answers to these questions, how to make sense of the pieces of this seemingly senseless jigsaw—God alone knows."

For at least one of the relatives of the dead, Bert Ammerman, an answer to those questions did come, and it came in a way that has made him begin a fight that is the consuming passion of his life.

7

THE CONSPIRACY—THE PFLP–GENERAL COMMAND IN GERMANY

"The PFLP-GC is a group with a record of fanatical attacks."

On an autumn day in 1988 four men were driving along Rhineside roads toward the largely industrial town of Neuss, across the river from Düsseldorf. Unknown to them, their car was being followed by agents of the West German security police, the BKA. Not far from the town the car was stopped and the four were arrested at gunpoint.

In a precisely coordinated operation across the Federal Republic, a number of apartments were being raided and known Palestinian sympathizers were being detained. An unoccupied apartment in Neuss was broken into by the BKA as other police were breaking in the door of number 28 Sandweg in the center of Frankfurt. It was the culmination of a West German surveillance operation that had been going on for many weeks.

One of the men stopped near Neuss on that day October 26 was forty-seven-year-old Hafez Kassan

Dalkamoni, suspected by the West German federal authorities of being the ringleader of a cell of the Popular Front for the Liberation of Palestine–General Command (PFLP–GC), the PLO splinter group headed by one of the world's most bloodthirsty terrorists, Ahmad Jabril.

Dalkamoni had been observed making regular visits to Frankfurt and Neuss from the Syrian capital, Damascus. Material found in his car and in the apartments in Neuss and Frankfurt convinced the BKA that an attack on an aircraft was in the final stages of planning. In the car they found a radio cassette recorder, a Toshiba BomBeat 453 that was primed with a small charge of Semtex explosive. The electronics of the machine had been replaced with a timing device connected to a barometric fuse.

In the apartment in Neuss a second Toshiba radio cassette recorder was found with other electrical equipment. This one had not been modified in any way, but the BKA believed it was awaiting the expert work to be done on it to make a second barometric bomb, a device that is designed to explode in an aircraft when it reaches a predetermined height, the lowering of atmospheric pressure at high altitude being the trigger that explodes it.

At the Sandweg apartment, where Dalkamoni and one of the other car passengers, Abdel Fatteh Ghadanfar, had been regular visitors, the police raid uncovered an arsenal of explosives and equipment, including a Beretta pistol with nine hundred rounds of ammunition and six Kalashnikov automatic rifles with nineteen magazines and three silencers. In addition, police recovered five kilos of Semtex, 5.87 kilos of another (unidentified) plastic explosive, three kilos of TNT, and eighty-nine detonators.

The four from the car were taken to Frankfurt for questioning, along with a further ten people detained in raids elsewhere. Those ten were released quite quickly for, despite the deep suspicion of the BKA, there was no evidence to link them with the weapons finds. Two from the car were also released later for lack of evidence, leaving only Dalkamoni and Ghadanfar in custody. As of this writing, they are still in custody and awaiting trial. The two released passengers were the owner of the flat in Neuss and Jordanian-born Marvan Kreesat. The BKA believed that Kreesat was the technician who made the bomb found in the car and that he was constructing the other devices found in Neuss. He was freed on appeal to a Frankfurt judge due to lack of evidence, and the West Germans believe he immediately fled to Syria.

It has since been claimed that Kreesat was a double agent working for West German security. Although this is strongly denied by the West Germans, it is clear that they do have a mole inside the PFLP-GC structure in the Federal Republic. The fourth, unnamed man in the car moved in Neuss after being arrested and released, and it was at his new apartment on April 13 that the BKA found three more bombs they had missed in the October raids (see Chapter 10).

Dalkamoni has admitted being a member of the PFLP-GC, but he claims that he was simply a finance officer of the terror group and, despite the materials recovered from his car, not involved in military operations. Ghadanfar claims only to have been Dalkamoni's assistant.

However, the BKA, armed with intelligence from security agencies outside West Germany, placed forty-seven-year-old Jordanian Dalkamoni at a much more central position within the PFLP-GC structure; they regard him as the mastermind behind the terrorist outrage that was clearly being planned from the Sandweg apartment.

Two conclusions were drawn by the BKA. First, it seemed clear that they had interrupted a plot to blow up an aircraft in mid-flight. The barometric fuse on the radio cassette recorder meant that it was designed solely for this purpose. If a hijacking was being considered by the PFLP-GC, they would not have gone to the trouble of constructing the barometric device that would trigger itself, once primed on the ground, without the need for a suicidal terrorist to be on the target aircraft.

The second and perhaps most important conclusion was that other members of the PFLP-GC cell had either slipped through the net for lack of hard evidence against them, or had not been picked up in the raids of October 26.

Western intelligence sources say that the downing of Flight 103 was positively linked to the Frankfurt cell within seventy-two hours of the crash, not just because of the obvious similarities in the bomb used, but also because of intelligence reports passed to the CIA by the Israeli secret service, Mossad, which has in the past claimed to have infiltrated every Palestinian terror organization in existence. In addition, the Israeli government's anti-terrorist adviser, Ygan Camone, had already tipped off the West German authorities that Mossad had uncovered evidence of a planned bomb attempt on an airliner out of Frankfurt.

The main Lockerbie inquiry, under the guidance of Detective Chief Superintendent John Orr, has actively

pursued lines of investigation connected with the
PFLP-GC cell. It is understood that in March 1989, at a
summit meeting of police chiefs in Bonn, Mr. Orr was
given permission to deploy surveillance teams in West
Germany to monitor the activities of suspected members
of the group. Because of these intelligence reports, and
because the PFLP-GC clearly had the capability of mounting a bomb attack on Pan Am 103, they have been identified by the police as the main suspects.

In classic detection work, after capability come two
other criteria: motive and opportunity.

The motives behind a PFLP-GC attack on a soft
American target are many, according to Dr. Bob Kupperman of the Institute of Strategic Studies in Washington, D.C. As a hard-line Palestinian organization, the
PFLP-GC are antagonistic toward the PLO, which is cur-
rently undergoing a rehabilitation from extreme terrorist
organization to credible negotiating force, suitable to deal
with over the future of an independent homeland for the
displaced Palestinian people. The fact that the PLO is
now in direct talks with Western governments, and that
there is now the possibility of talks between those two
former sworn enemies, Yasir Arafat and the Israeli government, is the cause of immense annoyance to the
PFLP-GC.

In addition, there are hardline factions (mainly the
Revolutionary Guards) within Iran that are opposed to
closer links between Iran and the West. Before 21 December 1988 and the air disaster (and before the trouble
caused by Salman Rushdie's novel *The Satanic Verses*),
there were clear signs of improvement in Iran's relations

with the West, an improvement that some within Iran
would want stopped. Then, and to some observers more
important, Iran could be motivated against the United
States by a desire to avenge the shooting down by the USS
Vincennes of their airbus carrying pilgrims to Mecca.

Dr. Kupperman says there is also a great deal of to-
ing and fro-ing among terrorist organizations, and a hybrid
of Palestinian and Iranian factions could have been responsible for the attempt.

The PLO itself has been somewhat put out by the
seeming lack of interest on the part of the Lockerbie investigators to talk to them in their new role as mainstream
political entity. The PLO has, however, conducted its own
inquiry into the Lockerbie disaster and, perhaps not sur-
prisingly, has pinned the blame on an old enemy Ahmad
Jabril, who broke away from the PLO in 1986. PLO officials privately say that Jabril's group made and planted the
bomb on flight 103 and were paid $10 million for their
trouble by Iran. The PLO goes further, stating that the
money was handed over to the PFLP-GC in Libya, drawing Colonel Ghadaffi into the scenario. Because of the en-
mity between the PLO and their former commander,
Jabril, it is clear that investigators in both Britain and
America would put little credibility on these claims if they
were not backed by hard evidence. (Jabril has publicly denied responsibility for the Lockerbie bombing.)

The world aviation industry and the government departments responsible for air travel have devised systems for
gathering intelligence on possible terrorist attacks on aircraft, and channels through which that intelligence is dis-

seminated to airline staff. Since the spate of hijackings in the 1970s and early 1980s, aircraft and airports are regarded as prime terrorist targets, and steps have been taken to try and defend them.

However, the raids in West Germany on October 26 sent shockwaves throughout the aviation community. Anti-terrorism expert Professor Paul Wilkinson of Aberdeen University says the reaction to the raids was quite fast, and so it should have been. "What was turned up in the raids in October in Frankfurt and elsewhere must have been the most serious basis of all on which to take very, very serious precautions [at airports]. This was not just a report from some Middle Eastern country. Here you had a discovery of a group with the very type of weapon which could do mayhem if it got into an airliner. The PFLC-GC is a group with a track record of fanatical attacks against Israeli or Western targets and certainly known to have a capability in Western countries, a cell structure in place. Here was the most serious ground, by itself, for a serious warning to carriers using Frankfurt Airport."

The BKA also knew, in the days that followed the arrest of Dalkamoni and Ghadanfar, that they had not "cracked" the case. They were fully aware of the possibility that further members of the PFLP-GC had escaped the net, and indeed, as late as April 1989, six months after the October raids, the West German authorities said that their investigation into other alleged members of the group in West Germany was still very active. Sources there say that the BKA believe that devices like the one found in Dalkamoni's car, and the one that police suspect brought down Pan Am 103, are still in circulation in that country.

In early November 1988, not long after the discovery of the barometric bomb and the one in the making at Neuss, the West Germans brought officials from the relevant departments of other European governments, including Britain, to Frankfurt to show them exactly what had been found.

Professor Wilkinson says this discovery should have been taken extremely seriously. "Evidence of what had been found was made known, so the West Germans cannot be criticized for trying to keep this information to themselves. They have a record of being conscientious about this sort of thing. This alone should have been enough to trigger a very precautionary mood among other countries, particularly the United States."

It is entirely likely that the materials found at the PFLP-GC apartments in West Germany were being stored for use in that country. The General Command is known to have cells of activists in many countries outside their adopted homeland of Syria, and there would be no reason for them to manufacture devices and store arms in West Germany for use anywhere else.

For example, Professor Wilkinson says that the PFLP-GC has certainly had people in the United States in the past. "And certainly they have people in other Western countries in various guises—businessmen and students, whatever—to set up an infrastructure in other countries.

"West Germany is a useful place to be, bearing in mind access to other countries through the airport system. Frankfurt is an attractive place for them to operate in. I think the GC uncovered in October were intending to use where they were found as their main area of operations. If they had wanted to act further afield, they would have used an infrastructure in France, Spain, England, and wherever."

The Professor says it's hard to guess what the hidden agenda was to have been, but the most likely chosen targets would have been people who were perceived as having taken action against the PFLP-GC. For instance, if the West German authorities had in jail someone they regarded as a hero, someone who needed to be sprung, that would be a reason for mounting an attack. Or it could have been punishment for West German action in cooperating with the United States or with Israel.

"Bear in mind," he says, "that these groups like PFLP-GC are linked, if only loosely, with other anti-American, anti-Zionist (in their terms) groups . . . so it is quite feasible for them to be utilizing the devices that were captured, not simply for pursuing a private PFLP-GC objective against America. For example, for initiating the discussion with Arafat, they would be against America for that, and for the *Vincennes* insofar as they feel common ground with Iranian fundamentalists in their bitter opposition to American policy in the Middle East.

"And remember: The Iranian fundamentalists have made common cause with the Palestinian rejectionists in rejecting any negotiated solution for the Palestine issue. And remember again, the Palestinian militants have become interested in the Iranian fundamentalists' success, as they see it.

"There has not been an integration, because that is very rare in terms of international terrorism, but there has been a coming together in the belief that certain tactics work—a mutual admiration for utilizing certain methods, and a mutual awareness of having 'common enemies,' which has led quite unlikely groups in the past to cooperate with one another."

One group did make a direct claim of responsibility for the downing of Flight 103. On the day after the crash, various London news agencies were telephoned by a caller saying he represented the "Guardians of the Islamic Revolution." He said that they bombed Flight 103 in direct retaliation for the downing of the Iran airbus on July 3. This claim was dismissed at the time.

However, at Aberdeen University, Professor Wilkinson is not so quick to dismiss the Guardians of the Islamic Revolution. "I think this claim was an interesting one and therefore should not be dismissed lightly. It's the sort of code name, or nom de guerre, that the fundamentalists use. It does not necessarily mean that they have a core of people that can go out and do this, but they may, nevertheless, be the people who claim the origin, the plan for doing it. It is not inconceivable that they are the expression, the visible and outward manifestation, of the fundamentalist link with the PFLP-GC."

Wilkinson says that the timing of the Flight 103 attack—four days before Christmas—is not insignificant when it is remembered that the downing of the Iranian airbus carrying Muslim pilgrims to Mecca occurred four days before their main religious holiday of the year. "To them, these dates and calendars are very important." And, Professor Wilkinson says, the importance given to dates by the terrorists is well known to intelligence agencies as they prepare security bulletins.

* * *

The next warning that went to the airline industry was the one that, as we have seen, causes the most anger among the relatives of those who died at Lockerbie. In many ways it is the strangest of them all.

On December 5, a man whose identity is still not conclusively known to police telephoned the U.S. Embassy in Helsinki to warn in broken English of a bombing attempt to be made, he said, against a Pan Am flight from Frankfurt.

The caller named two Palestinians who, he claimed, were behind the plot. A Finnish woman would be tricked into carrying an aircraft bomb from Helsinki to Frankfurt sometime in the next fourteen days and would then board a Pan Am flight bound for the United States.

The caller said that the individuals he had named were part of the Abu Nidal terror group, but he would not elucidate on the source of his information. The U.S. Embassy contacted the Finnish security police and were told, in general terms, that the call was most likely a hoax. The reason for discounting the warning was that three almost identical calls had been made to the Israeli Embassy in Helsinki during 1988. However, the security police investigated this latest warning and interviewed the man named in it. They were satisfied that Mr. Gabadat had no connection with any terrorist organization, and they believed that the call had been made because of a feud among Palestinians living in Finland, a feud probably of a personal nature.

Despite this information, the U.S. Embassy in Helsinki appears to have given some credence to the warning, in as much as staff there passed word of it through State

Department channels to the Federal Aviation Administration, which regulates American airlines.

The FAA receives hundreds of intelligence reports each year, and they are all dealt with in the same manner. Officials from the FAA, the Defense Intelligence Agency, and other federal bodies have formed a committee that considers each report. When they think it appropriate, they disseminate the information in unclassified form in a security bulletin to airlines. As a matter of routine, the bulletins are also passed to other relevant air-regulatory bodies the world over, and in Britain that means the Department of Transport and, through them, the Civil Aviation Authority.

On December 7 the Federal Aviation Administration issued the first of two warning bulletins on the Helsinki warning. It was coded "ACS 88 22"—indicating that it was the twenty-second such warning notice of 1988. It was released under the name of Raymond Salazar, the FAA's leading anti-terrorism advisor.

As is usual in the case of warnings issued by the FAA, officials added what they call a "commentary," a guide as to how the information should be handled. For the Helsinki warning, the FAA commentary was:

> The reliability of the information cannot be assessed at this point. The appropriate police authorities have been advised and are persuing [sic] the matter. Pan American is also aware of the threat information. As reported in FAA Security Bulletins ACS 88 19 and ACS 88 20, terrorist groups continue to target civil aviation, at times with the use of sophisticated im-

provised explosive devices (IED) that may be very difficult to detect during screening. Unwitting couriers have also been employed in the past.

In notes at the bottom of the bulletin, the FAA said that this information must be passed to all U.S. couriers and to U.S. airlines with international routes. In a separate note to the State Department, the FAA stated that the contents of ACS 88 22 "may be disseminated to appropriate U.S. Foreign Service posts, which should refer for guidance to Secstate."

The reason for the anger of the relatives of those who died at Lockerbie is the fact that the contents of the Helsinki warning were disclosed to some U.S. government employees. On December 13 a memo concerning it was pinned to the wall of the staff canteen in the U.S. Embassy in Moscow.

Months later, at a U.S. Senate hearing into the Lockerbie crash, Ambassador Clayton E. McManaway of the State Department told the five Senators in public session: "By December tenth the Finnish police had determined the 'threat' was a hoax. The U.S. fully concurred in that judgment. In the wake of the Pan Am bombing, this 'threat' was thoroughly reinvestigated by the Finns, the U.S., and other concerned governments. It is our unanimous conclusion that the Helsinki 'threat' was baseless."

In addition, in a letter to a relative of one of the victims, Pan Am Chairman Thomas G. Plaskett wrote that, on December 6, "Law enforcement officials in Finland determined [the Helsinki warning] to be a hoax."

On 21 March 1989, in the House of Commons, U.K.

Transport Secretary Channon sought to bury the Helsinki warning once and for all. He told Members of Parliament that the FAA had issued a warning bulletin on the Helsinki threat that had been received by the Department of Transport on December 9.

"My department immediately had the information in the bulletin assessed in conjunction with the appropriate United States authorities: the conclusion was that the information contained therein had little credibility. My department decided that, for the moment, no further measures were necessary in the light of the bulletin. Special security measures were already in force in respect of United States flights out of the United Kingdom."

In response to a supplementary question from Labor leader Neil Kinnock, Channon went further: ". . . the reason we gave no credence to the Helsinki warning was that it was not worthy of any. The American government do not think it worthy of credence, nor do the Finnish government. The Lockerbie investigators are not following up any trails relating to that warning in their inquiry."

So just what is it that leaves no doubt whatsoever that the Helsinki warning was a hoax? After all, the caller had said that a Pan Am flight from Frankfurt to the United States would be bombed within two weeks. And a Pan Am flight from Frankfurt to the United States was blown out of the sky two weeks and two days after that warning was delivered.

McManaway said that by December 10 the U.S. was confident the warning was a hoax. Yet three days later U.S. Embassy staff in Moscow and elsewhere were being warned not to fly Pan Am from Frankfurt.

The investigation of the Helsinki warning fell to Seppo Tiidenen, chief of the security police in Finland. Tiidenen says that three calls of a similar nature were made to the Israeli Embassy in Helsinki naming a certain individual as the "alleged perpetrator" of a Frankfurt bomb plot. This man, already known to police, was thoroughly investigated. He was of Arab extraction, and, says Tiidenen, it was established that he had no links with terrorism. Further, says the police chief, they concluded that the threats to the Israeli Embassy had been made because of a dispute over a woman between the so-called "bomber" and the caller.

When the December 5 warning came to the U.S. Embassy in similar terms, the old ground was gone over once more and the old conclusions reached. To be sure that the threat really was a hoax, especially after it transpired to have been largely (if unwittingly) correct, the police needed to identify the person who made the call. This, according to Tiidenen, has not been done. He says: "We have heavy suspicions but no real evidence."

It is that admission, and the action taken following the threat, that leaves the Helsinki question one of the main unsatisfactory areas behind the Lockerbie disaster.

Police from Scotland spent considerable time in Helsinki, presumably going over the previous investigation and carrying out new inquiries. John Orr says that, at the moment, he has no evidence to suggest that the Helsinki warning is connected to his inquiry.

It is still not clear if, at any time, the U.S. Federal Aviation Administration canceled the security alerts sparked off by the Helsinki warning.

Paul Wilkinson says that as far as he is concerned, Helsinki cannot be ruled out of the equation. "If they can't be convinced who made the call, I would have thought it would be at least an open matter of judgment as to whether the thing was credible or not.

"You would not dismiss it unless you were absolutely sure the person who made the call was a well-known nutcase with no connection to terrorism. If you are not certain it was a hoaxer, you do not put out firm information that it was a hoax—you leave the thing open.

"One can see why it was convenient to people in the States and in Britain to say it was absolutely of no substance at all. Because it was so specific in form [and] if it had had substance, it would have revealed the inadequate reaction that was made to the warning.

"However, we now know there is no absolutely concrete evidence to pin that specific warning on a particular individual which would lead one to dismiss it. It is at least feasible that the Helsinki warning was made by someone who really did have inside knowledge of what was going to be done."

8

BRITAIN'S BIGGEST
MURDER HUNT

"Those responsible for tracking down the killers face
pressure from above."

Exactly one week after Pan Am clipper *Maid of the Seas*
had exploded at 31,000 feet over Lockerbie and crashed
on the town with such devastating effect, the Air Accident
Investigation Branch (AAIB) of the Department of Transport confirmed what most had suspected all along. It had
been a bomb.

Forensic analysis of luggage from the cargo hold of
the 747, along with detailed tests on the licoricelike substances that had been found days before at Carruthers
Farm, left no doubt that the plane had been blown out of
the sky by a bomb containing plastic explosives of some
kind. The indications were that it was Semtex.

At a news conference in the Masonic Hall, next to the
police station and just a few hundred yards from the devastation of Sherwood Crescent, the senior investigating officer of the AAIB, Mick Charles, said: "The explosive's
residues recovered from the debris have been positively
identified and are consistent with the use of a high-performance plastic explosive."

The confirmation came two days after a suitcase from the plane had been sent to the Royal Armament Research and Development establishment at Fort Halstead in Kent. It is thought, but cannot be proved at the moment, that the case marked with the vital evidence was that of Charles McKee, the case that had caused the CIA so many problems.

Mick Charles said they had concluded that the explosion had occurred soon after the plane had crossed the Scottish border. He also revealed that the metalwork from one particular luggage container showed conclusive proof of a high-performance explosive. "Much investigation work remains to be done to establish the nature of the explosive device, what it was contained in, its location in the aircraft, and the sequence of events immediately following detonation."

By the time of the news that it had been a bomb had been confirmed, police searches had recovered 241 bodies from in and around the town. They had also managed to establish exactly how many people on the ground had died. The burned-out cars found near the A74, which police feared had contained motorists vaporized by the blast, were discovered to have been blown to their resting places from Sherwood Crescent, where they had been parked. A number of people from that area had "come back from the dead," according to the popular press. In fact, they had been away on vacation on the night of the crash and only heard of the disaster on returning to Britain.

Police were coming to the conclusion that some bodies and wreckage might never be recovered, and would lie out on remote hills and difficult countryside for years to come.

The southwesterly gale of December 21 had blown wreckage more than forty miles across the border into England and through the Kielder Forest. At the same time as soldiers from Otterburn Camp were conducting line searches in an attempt to discover the evidence so desired by the CIA, Superintendent John Bowyer was in charge of searching an area of eighty-four square miles at Kielder. It was one of the most difficult operations, for the police officers had to slash their way through ranks of conifers so thick that some wreckage trapped high up in the trees and clearly visible from the air was impossible to see from the ground. For Superintendent Bowyer's officers, it was a daily battle against high winds, rain, and mist that often cut visibility down to just fifty yards. More than one policeman got lost in those difficult days.

They were assisted, like the police at Lockerbie, by many civilian volunteers. Ian Findlay, the leader of the Upper Teesdale & Weardale Fell Rescue Team, describes how the tragedy came home to him when he found a South African passport in the woods.

"I opened it and saw the picture of a pretty twenty-three-year-old girl looking out at me. As I held it, the thought crossed my mind that the last person to have touched it would have been the owner herself as she packed it into her handbag before boarding the plane.

"It was also upsetting to find children's clothing. The thought of how these had been worn recently by young people whose lives had suddenly been finished made us all choke."

* * *

Confirmation of a bomb on Flight 103 brought immense relief to Boeing, manufacturers of the 747, and partial relief to the world's airlines that employ the jet as the workhorse of mass air transport. They had feared that if a structural defect had been found to be the cause of the Lockerbie disaster, the effect on international air travel could be immense. Most of the big airlines had already cleared maintenance hangars for immediate overhauls of their 747 fleets, and tentative inquiries had been made to try and secure other wide-bodied aircraft, like DC-10's, to replace the jumbos taken out of service. A bomb meant that all those contingency plans could be dropped and life could go on as before.

However, the 259 killed over Lockerbie added up to yet another grim statistic for the airline industry to grapple with.

It had long been the view of air-security chiefs that bomb attacks on aircraft, designed to cripple the plane and kill all those aboard, were not a major threat. It was the perceived wisdom of the industry that terrorists are not fanatical enough to make suicide attacks on aircrafts. Yet the people killed in Lockerbie took the total crew and passengers killed by bombs on planes to 738 in just three and a half years:

● June 1985: 329 people died when an Air India flight crashed into the Atlantic off Ireland, killing all on board.

● March 1986: four people died when a bomb exploded

on a TWA Boeing 727 approaching Athens on a flight to Cairo. The jet managed to land.

● May 1986: thirty-one people died when a bomb exploded in an Air Lanka jet on the tarmac at the Colombo airport in Sri Lanka.

● November 1987: 115 people died when Korean Airlines Flight 707 was destroyed over Burma with the loss of all on board.

It was slowly dawning on the security chiefs that the day of the hijack was receding in favor of mass murder.

It is entirely likely that even though the identity of the bomber of Flight 103 is not known to the Lockerbie investigators, the various intelligence agencies that are giving them "full cooperation" have identified the group and the main individuals who hatched the plan and saw it through to execution.

That proposition is supported by two facts. First there was the controversy over the widely reported off-the-record remarks made by U.K. Transport Secretary Paul Channon at a private lunch with five journalists (remarks he later disputed) that the identity of the bomber was known to the police and that an arrest was imminent. Second and more important, permission was sought by John Orr at a "summit" meeting with West German authorities in March 1989 to deploy surveillance teams to watch suspects in that country. British Foreign Secretary Sir Geoffrey Howe confirmed suspicions of the Middle Eastern origin of the Lockerbie bombing by calling on governments in that region to help track down the bomber.

One of the international dimensions to the inquiry in the immediate aftermath of the bomb revelations was the desire of the American people for revenge. Libya had been bombed, in error as it turned out, for a bomb attack on a Berlin disco that had killed one U.S. national. In the Lockerbie disaster the United States had seen the slaughter of more than 160 of its citizens. President-elect George Bush vowed to seek out and punish those responsible for the "cowardly attack" at Lockerbie, but refused to elaborate on what might or might not be done.

This means that those responsible for tracking down the killers face pressure from above that will be far in excess of anything a senior police officer could expect in the normal run of detective work. John Orr is widely regarded as a man who will not allow such pressures to deflect him from his main task of identifying those responsible for Lockerbie. The forty-three-year-old Orr has spent most of his twenty years in the force as a detective. The reason he landed the toughest job in British police history is part accident—he is thought, although no one will confirm this, to have simply been the senior officer on call on December 21—and part recognition of his qualities as a detective. He is a quiet and patient man, steeped in the Scottish way of policing, with an ability to motivate the officers beneath him. In his spare time he followed, and passed, an Open University course in social sciences, and took a postgraduate degree in forensic science. His mem-

The cockpit of *Maid of the Seas*. The bomb went off right at the rear part of this section. Searchers say that whilst the cockpit appears to be largely intact, the bodies inside were horrifically mutilated.

Above: One of the larger pieces of wreckage lying in fields above Lockerbie.

Right: Another body is loaded into the rear of an army ambulance in the field near Tundergarth church.

One of the enduring mysteries of Lockerbie is how Ella Ramsden managed to get alive and unscathed from this house. Her goldfish, budgie, and dog also survived. Mrs Ramsden lived – the bodies of more than seventy people were found in her house and garden, many of them students of Syracuse University.

Above: An aerial view of the Sherwood estate; in the foreground are the A74 and the crater. The roofless houses were blown apart by the exploding aviation fuel – the explosion measured 1.9 on the Richter earthquake scale.

Right: A seat from Flight 103 comes to rest in the upper window of one of the houses on the Rosebank estate.

One of the houses in Sherwood Crescent that burst into flames with the intense heat of the explosion nearby.

Above: Charles H Price, the American ambassador, and Mrs Price, arriving at disaster control HQ on the morning of December 22.

Left: Prince Andrew, Duke of York, faces the press after his gruesome tour of the disaster area. His comments at Lockerbie earned him the nickname 'The Second Lockerbie Disaster'.

Mrs Thatcher offers comfort to the townsfolk after arriving in Lockerbie within twenty hours of the crash. This time the royals managed to beat her to the scene of national mourning.

bership in Rotary International allowed him to spend two months in the United States studying police methods in Kansas and Oklahoma.

Orr had another advantage. He has been positively vetted to high levels of security clearance, making him a suitable recipient of intelligence gathered by, or handed to, the British Secret Intelligence Service.

9

THE BEREAVED

"Why did they try to deny me comfort?"

The growing number of American relatives arriving in Lockerbie were wandering around the town almost in a daze. Desperate for information, they had nothing to keep them occupied, and they were anxious to help if they could.

They took solace in each other's company. There were long conversations centered on the sharing of grief, the pooling of knowledge. Eventually, Paul Hudson, a New York lawyer and father of sixteen-year-old Melina, asked police if they could arrange a daily briefing for the relatives to keep them informed. That request was readily agreed to, and every afternoon at three o'clock Dumfries Deputy Chief Constable Paul Newell met the relatives in an upstairs art room at Lockerbie Academy to tell them of the latest developments.

Some people in Lockerbie feel that they were almost deliberately kept away from the American relatives. Ballet school teacher Maureen Scott talks of a desire felt by many townsfolk to reach out and help, to share their side of the story of the disaster.

That feeling was reciprocated. Carolyn Ammerman wanted to help during the ten days she spent in Lockerbie, to feel that she was doing something useful. She ended up working twelve hours a day in the canteen, helping to provide meals for emergency workers and refreshments for her fellow Americans. There was a huge bond of goodwill between the townsfolk and the grieving foreigners. One U.S. visitor remarked casually that she was surprised there was no shortbread being served with the coffee in the relatives' lounge. She thought everyone in Scotland ate shortbread. News of this spread around the town, and within hours there was sufficient shortbread, home-baked and bought from the shops, to build a wall.

In Lockerbie it was the children of preteen years who were affected by the crash more than most. There are still, as of this writing, those who have difficulty sleeping. It was just as they went to bed that Wednesday night before Christmas that the terrible noise and subsequent explosion was heard around the town.

A group of youngsters were talking before one of Maureen Scott's classes. She deliberately left the room so she could eavesdrop and hear what their shared reaction to the crash had been. Strangely, they sat and tried to scare each other with ghost stories. Many children in the town still overreact to loud noises. It does not take much to take their young minds back to the night of December 21.

As each day passed, more bodies were found, more identified, more released to the relatives. Residents of the town were acutely aware that bodies were constantly being moved around the town. It was a creepy feeling.

Bert Ammerman says that he and the other Americans continued to try to find out more information. "We'd go to Pan Am, the police, anyone, and find out what we could and then try and piece it together. In addition, I'd go out each day and walk 'round the town trying to find out more. I sneaked into Sherwood Crescent on Christmas Eve to see the damage and devastation and talk to the people on the street there, to try and get an idea of what was going on. We felt on our own though. We had to go out and find out for ourselves."

On Christmas Eve, Bert and his six relatives went to the midnight mass at the Catholic church and were deeply impressed with the service. "Six of us were Catholic, one wasn't, but he wanted to stay with us. It was very emotional. The bishop made a homily that was carried by television all 'round the world.

"Christmas Day was just like any other day. It lost its significance. At eight o'clock on the morning I was in the relatives' lounge as usual, trying to get information. Phoning home to tell the rest of the family what was going on. It was just an intense day of gathering information, and the day itself didn't really have an impact on me. About three days later it really hit me. I remembered that I hadn't even bothered to ask the children back home what they got for Christmas."

Bert Ammerman made a decision not to return to New Jersey until either his brother's body was found or it was certain that it was not going to be found. "I would have stayed even if it had taken two months, or three months. I was able to bring Tommy home on January second."

Relatives who stayed in the United States were less able to keep in touch with what was happening in Lockerbie. Mrs. Doris Coker, whose twin stepsons, twenty-year-olds Eric and Jason, died on the plane, complained that every time she phoned the State Department for information, none was forthcoming.

One night, in desperation, Mrs. Coker phoned the Lockerbie police station. The officer who answered the phone could not help her but undertook to call her back. Weeks later Mrs. Coker told a Senate hearing into the disaster that she had been phoned back twenty minutes later with the answer she was looking for. That made her ring more often, and each time, her transatlantic question was answered within minutes.

Mrs. Judy Papadopolous is more stark in her appraisal of the State Department: "Our State Department are pigs."

All over the Eastern seaboard families that had never met were finding they had something in common—grief.

Mark Tobin's father, Joe, fought back tears as he looked down a provisional list of the dead in the *New York Times*. He noticed an unusual name among them: "Tsairis, Alexia Kathryn, aged twenty." The people who lived just a few doors away were called Tsairis. "Their son is a surgeon in New York," recalled Mr. Tobin. "I wonder . . ."

He called a hospital. He found out where Dr. Tsairis worked. He called him. Within seconds the two grieving fathers were crying their eyes out over the phone. Eventually they became so emotional that they had to hang up.

After leaving Kennedy Airport, Dan and Susan Cohen drove to their house and to their daughter Theodora's room, which would now forever remain empty. Mrs. Cohen, who had already tried to throw herself out of the car twice on the way to the airport, now found the will to go on. Neighbors, friends, relatives, all rallied to support the Cohens. Friends of their daughter from Syracuse University came to their home and slept on the living room floor so that the couple would not be alone. The Christmas tree that had been too festive, too cheerful to bear, was quietly taken down and put away.

It was a story being repeated in dozens of homes. Neighbors arrived with meals, phone calls of introduction came from other bereaved, wanting to share, to help. Friendships were formed in those hours and days after the crash that will last forever.

"In the middle of all this ghastly evil," says Mrs. Cohen, "there is a beautiful side to people, and it has come out."

Bert Ammerman has an almost spiritual feeling about Flight 103. It is almost as though, he says, God chose the people who would die.

"It seems to have been a flight of fate. The worst thing I ever heard anyone say about Tommy was that he was a nice guy. No one ever had a bad word to say about him. He was basically a fantastic person, a laid-back guy who would give you the shirt off his back. He knew what he wanted, but he was not a person who would like to get into controversy or be confrontational if he could possibly avoid it.

"As you talk to more and more of the relatives of people on that flight, they all seem to fit that mold. They are the all-American boy or girl, the all-British boy or girl, or whatever. The devoted spouse, the loving father or mother. Really, truly, when you listen to it, it seems to be like a flight of fate that brought these people together to be used as a tool or as a cause to help other people." It was this feeling, obviously shared by many of the relatives, that has been the driving force behind their subsequent campaigning.

Lynda Mack was the person who had intervened in Elizabeth Dix's near fight with the embassy official on Christmas Eve. A twenty-seven-year-old student studying for a doctorate at Cambridge University, Lynda Mack had been in Lockerbie since the day before, trying to find out what had happened to her friend, Julian Benello, the brilliant American researcher from Brookline, Massachusetts, who had been at King's College, Cambridge. She had been surprised when, at the last minute, Julian had been able not only to get a seat on the flight, but also to buy a half-price ticket.

"I felt that I had cared for him in life and now I wanted to care for him in death. I wanted to know whether or not his body had been found, if it had been destroyed in the crater at Sherwood Crescent.

"I wanted to be told if his clothes had been discovered. Could I see him? If not, could I possibly touch his covered body? Or sit by the coffin? I did not get one answer in two weeks of going to the Academy every morning and sitting there until seven P.M. There was a daily police briefing that told us nothing.

"I must have given his description to police, airline officials, embassy staff, thirty times. It was cheapening, it made him seem worthless. I kept thinking they had lost Julian's details or not bothered to write them down."

Mrs. Dix was visited on January 20 by Scotland Yard

police officers collecting details of the movements of her husband Peter. During the friendly questions, they let drop that Peter's body had been found on December 22. This was a bombshell for Mrs. Dix because the authorities had not informed her until New Year's Day.

On New Year's Day her priest and doctor had gone to Lockerbie to see the body. At first they were not going to be allowed to see it because they were not next of kin, but eventually they were.

"The doctor and the priest gave me my only moment of peace, almost of quiet joy, because they told me that Peter was not badly burned. He was absolutely visible as himself, lying there with his curly hair and his moustache, and his face was at rest.

"For me there will be no more nightmares or visions of disfigurement. Why did they try to deny me that comfort? Why did they spend eleven days withholding information when my family could have been saved having to ask every day if his body had been found? Our family wanted to come together and mourn as one. We wanted quietly to cherish Peter. What they did to us, the obstructions they raised, denied us that. It never happened for us and it never will."

Harsher criticisms were to be directed at police. The most damning came from Pan Am pilot Bruce Smith, whose wife Ingrid had died in the crash. "My contacts with Dumfries and Galloway police over the past week," said Captain Smith at the turn of the year, "have convinced me that they reach the upper limit of their competence directing traffic and issuing parking tickets. They are so paralyzed by incompetence or inexperience that they have not even released the body of the pilot to his family, despite the fact he was found some days ago and identified by Pan Am colleagues."

The criticism was understandable, and publicly supported by other relatives, who were also angry at the time taken to return property recovered from the bodies and luggage of their loved ones. It was, however, unfounded, and Captain Smith and the others would have realized this if only they had stopped to think about it. It has to be remembered that, by January 1 police were dealing with 242 bodies, many beyond all hope of identification. They were dealing with 270 cases of murder. In the early days every single person on the plane must have been under suspicion of having carried on the explosive device. Bodies and possessions all yielded vital evidence. They could not be released until thoroughly examined and checked for clues. Once released, anything they may have been able to add to the investigation would be lost forever.

In an attempt to quell the criticism, police mounted a unique exercise. In March, Deputy Chief Constable Paul Newell, Superintendent Angus Kennedy, the inquiry press officer, and two other senior officers flew to the United States and conducted a series of group meetings with relatives to explain the delays and to answer questions. They even took color slides of the area around Lockerbie to show the difficulties that the police were up against and to give relatives an idea of where their loved ones had come to rest.

These meetings were all packed, extremely emotional, and often went on for many hours. After each one the anger was diffused, transformed into admiration and praise.

During her time in Lockerbie, Lynda Mack started asking questions. Why were there so many empty seats on the plane? Was it the Helsinki warning, relayed to diplomats, that had allowed some people to cancel their flight and save their lives? Why was Pan Am—by Christmas, already threatened with negligence suits—being allowed to shepherd the American relatives so closely when they came to Lockerbie? Lynda's questions were shared by other relatives and friends of the dead. For the moment, though, there was the business of death to get on with.

Eventually, when funerals had been held, when the grieving process was under way and normality, while never being able to return fully, was at least in sight, those questions came back. And, fueled by their anger at the delays in the return of property, relatives started banding together. The main mover in that was Paul Hudson. He had been pursuing officials in the weeks after his daughter's death, trying to set his mind at rest. Like so many of the relatives, he received little satisfaction, and so, on February 19, the "Victims of Pan Am Flight 103" group was launched. The purpose of the group was manyfold: to speed the return of the belongings, to receive answers to questions, to press for a full independent investigation into Pan Am 103 in particular and air security in general.

The inaugural meeting, in New Jersey, attracted a crowd of American press. The memories of the disaster were only just beginning to fade in the minds of the public, so it did not take much to rekindle media interest and thus help the cause.

Over the next few days various committees were formed: a legal one to press for compensation, a political one to press for the inquiry; a financial one to help raise funds for the fight; and one to give emotional support.

The chairman of the political committee, Bert Ammerman, has become a powerful advocate for the cause. He has shown an ability to present exactly the right amount of emotion, always backed up with fact, and has persuaded many members of the United States Senate to back their cause.

"It is obvious the organization we formed can only be a reflection of the people on the flight. The organization has refused to stop until we have the appropriate action take place to find out why this happened, and the appropriate changes take place to ensure this does not happen again, until we have the changes necessary in airport security. If those changes do take place, then we will become more of a support group and moderate its intensity and try to direct ourselves to helping each other. We're trying to do this at the moment, but we can't because we are still in the political arena."

Bert Ammerman will admit to being obsessed by the circumstances surrounding Flight 103. It may be, for him, as much a personal need as a public crusade. He admits that while he is carrying out the fight, his brother is still alive.

In Britain, Lynda Mack and Elizabeth Dix have been leading the fight to unearth information surrounding Flight 103. Lynda Mack is involved to such an extent that she has now abandoned her doctorate and hopes that the fight she is waging may help her obtain a career in journalism.

Bert Ammerman says that the more he finds out each day, the more he realizes this should never have happened. "Certain factions of us are angry, but that is an extreme statement. We are more frustrated, disappointed in the different agencies, at the way in which our government has approached it.

"I think, periodically, as you get more information, the anger comes out, but then you realize, government to government, this is not unusual. Perhaps we just held our government in too high esteem. What has made us successful is that we do not show a lot of emotion. We just state the facts in the best way possible, and that has impressed a lot of people."

Dumfries social-work director Tom McMenamay says that his staff were somewhat apprehensive of the imminent arrival of the American relatives in Lockerbie. They, of course, knew how people in Britain responded to these events, but they were, to an extent, dealing with the unknown with their transatlantic visitors.

"Having said we would offer them support and care . . . I was determined these would not just be words. Especially for folks traveling all those thousands of miles. It was important I had social workers there to meet them to help them as they arrived in a place they had no idea of. Really it was just to say hello and offer what help we could.

"My staff stayed with them all the time they were there, to give them immediate and available support and what information we could. A lot of people wanted to know the exact spot their loved ones died at, but it wasn't possible for us to help them. There was a lot of bonding between social worker and relative. They really became friends."

McMenamay took the view that it was unlikely that people would be allowed to see bodies, but it seemed to him that if they could not, it would be detrimental to their coping with the grief. "It is part of our culture to see the body, and that gives evidence of death. Lots of folks go through life and never see a dead person and find it hard to come to terms with the fact there has been death.

"If [seeing the body] is not possible, you have to see something that reinforces the impact of death. My people were able to at least take relatives around the various sites, and that helped."

Many of the relatives decided in their own minds the exact spots where their loved ones came to rest and treated them almost as graves. Many put flowers on the spot and photographed it. One policeman at Tundergarth remembers an Indian woman trying to plant a rose bush near the cockpit. He managed to persuade her that the field would be ploughed soon, and instead the bush was planted in the nearby graveyard.

Wednesday, 4 January 1989, marked two weeks after the disaster. In Lockerbie's ice rink thirty police officers sat in silence, their eyes fixed on a television screen in the officers' room on the first floor. The image that held their attention was of a congregation packed into the town's Dryfesdale Parish Church, its austere Presbyterian interior brightly illuminated by the lights of the world's television cameras. A room away a ringing phone went unanswered as the police officers, relieved for a morning of the worst ordeal of their lives, watched the memorial service for the 270 people who had died above and in the town.

Their concentration on the television was disrupted by an irate chief inspector berating them for failing to answer the phone. "If it happens again, that television's going off," he warned. The muttered dissent from the audience made the uniformed officer turn away in the sure knowledge that the phone would indeed be allowed to go unanswered and that turning off the set would be an unwise course of action.

Outside, the gray January clouds were drizzling on the great, the good, the bereaved, and the ordinary folk of Scotland who had come to pay their respects. The town, which had seen tremendous activity in its streets in the previous two weeks, had fallen silent. Those who could not get into the church stood in its graveyard. When the graveyard was full, they stood on the streets.

In the bingo-hall-cum-cinema, and in the church halls, pictures and sound from the service were relayed to yet more of the townsfolk and people from all over Scotland and northern England.

The minister, the Rev. Jim Annand, remembers suddenly becoming aware part way through the service of how unreal it all had become. Looking down from the front of his church, where he had stood so many times before, he saw a completely new—and, two weeks previously, unthinkable—sight. The old ladies and families who usually occupied his pews had been replaced by the Prime

Minister, the Transport Secretary, the Scottish Secretary, the Labor leader Neil Kinnock, the U.S. Ambassador, the Lord Lieutenant. In his twenty-three years as parish minister he had not seen such a sight, nor even imagined it, let alone wanted to.

It had been decided to hold the memorial service sooner rather than later, as though the town wanted to get it over with and start anew. But the people huddled together and sheltering under umbrellas from the cold drizzle outside the television shop opposite the church knew that nothing could ever be the same again.

As the chauffeurs opened car doors to disgorge their passengers, there was not the usual face-spotting from the crowd. For once the famous were merely additions to the event. None would be feeling the cold of that Scottish January morning more than the Transport Secretary, Paul Channon, just back from the Caribbean and browned. It was a suntan that was not admired by many of the emergency workers down from the hills for a morning's respite.

In the minutes before the two P.M. ecumenical service, news circulated among the huge media representation that the Americans had shot down two Libyan fighters over the Mediterranean. It was news that the townsfolk felt strangely a part of. Could it be the start of the retaliation many thought inevitable after the bombing of Flight 103?

As the seven-hundred-strong congregation inside the church, and many more outside, sang the Twenty-third Psalm, there was an unspoken realization that together they had walked through the Valley of the Shadow of Death. They had come out of it largely unscathed. They

were there to remember those who had died. The cost had
been dear. Just why that price had to be paid was not clear
then, is not now, and probably never will be.

The main address of the service was given by the
Moderator of the General Assembly of the Church of
Scotland, the Very Rev. Professor James Whyte. His message of hope had an added poignancy for those who knew
of his own recent loss: his wife, who had died just a short
time before.

"When we cry in our pain," he said in his powerful,
softly accented voice, "we cry to one who knows pain, who
shares it with us. That is strange comfort, and it does not
take away our pain, but it may give it meaning as with a
flash of light.

"It is not only pain and grief we feel in this disaster,
but indignation. For this was not an unforeseeable natural
disaster such as an earthquake. Nor was it a result of human error or carelessness. This we now know was an act
of human wickedness. That such carnage of the young and
of the innocent should have been willed by men in cold
and calculating evil is horror upon horror.

"What is our response to that?

"The desire, the determination, that those who did
this should be detected and, if possible, brought to justice,
is natural and is right. The uncovering of the truth will not
be easy, and evidence that would stand up in a court of
law may be hard to obtain.

"Justice is one thing. But already one hears in the
media the word 'retaliation.' As far as I know, no responsible politician has used that word, and I hope none ever
will, except to disown it. For that way lies the endless cycle

of violence upon violence, horror upon horror. And we may be tempted, indeed urged by some, to flex our muscles in response, to show that we are men. To show that we are what? To show that we are prepared to let more young and more innocent die, to let more rescue workers labor in more wreckage to find the grisly proof, not of our virility, but of our inhumanity. That is what retaliation means. I, for one, will have none of it, and I hope you will not either . . .

"But there has been not only suffering here, there has been courage and sacrifice and understanding and compassion. A whole community reaching out with open hearts and open homes and willing hands to sustain and comfort those who have suffered loss. Rescue workers, soldiers, RAF, police, and civilians ready to work their hearts out to see what can be recovered from the wreckage. A coordination of essential services and of pastoral care so that those whose lives and homes have been shattered here, and those who have made the long, sad journey across the Atlantic, may be met with sensitive understanding and generous support and care."

The Moderator's words on retaliation were written well before news of the air attack on the Libyan fighters had reached Scotland. They were thought, by many, to be falling on deaf ears, not in Lockerbie, but across the ocean in Washington, where politicians might not allow such an outrage against their people to go without retaliation. But among those who had come to Dryfesdale Parish Church to mourn, the message had struck home with force and won universal support.

The emotions that had been held in during the forty-

minute service came to the surface as the people filed out
into the drizzle. Many of the American relatives broke
down in tears and sobbed as they dodged reporters and
headed back to the buses that had brought them to the
church. They went back to the Academy for tea. The
Prime Minister arrived with her sympathy, which she
shared for another forty minutes.

The end of the service was not the end of the day's
labor for the disaster workers. As Mrs. Thatcher's car sped
out of the town, it was time for everyone to get back to
work. For the media the next event was the first of the
funerals of those who had been killed on the ground.
There was a media briefing at four o'clock for the funeral
of ten-year-old Joanne Flannigan, which was to take place
the next day. Hers was the only body pulled out of the
wreckage at the immediate site of the crash at Sherwood
Crescent. There were camera positions to think about,
and sound feeds to agree on, so that the next stage of the
tragedy at Lockerbie could be relayed to the world without
a hitch.

In the Masonic Hall press officer Superintendent
Angus Kennedy sorted out the media inquiries and problems, making sure that everyone got the shots they needed
without encroaching on the funeral. The best vantage
point was to be behind the cemetery wall just a few yards
from the graveside. In the view of the press, Kennedy was
very professional.

And as for Scotland's new Lord Advocate, Peter Fraser, appointed only that morning, there was to be a very
personal conclusion to the end of his first day in office. His
aunt and uncle live at number 11 Sherwood Crescent.

They had been unhurt in the disaster, although their house suffered some damage. Their nephew was to visit them.

Joanne Flannigan's funeral, the morning after the memorial service, again brought the town to a standstill. In the afternoon Mary Lancaster, another Sherwood resident, was laid to rest. On the same day, at Tundergarth churchyard, Peter Dix was buried, just yards from where he had fallen from the sky before Christmas.

Seventeen people were still unaccounted for, ten from the plane and seven residents. Their bodies were not actually missing; they had either disintegrated, been blown apart by the explosion, or had been vaporized by the heat of the Sherwood explosion. At the ice-rink mortuary there were seventy bags containing parts of bodies that were not identifiable other than as human remains. There were also two coffins containing substantial portions of two bodies, again completely beyond identification.

It was decided to have these remains cremated. To help relatives of those seventeen people still unaccounted for, a special service would be held, and the ashes interred in Dryfesdale churchyard in a sort of "grave of the unknown victim."

As preparations were being made for the ceremony, mortuary officials discovered, to their horror, a second blunder with the bodies, one that, this time, would not be so easy to resolve. The two coffins had been opened, and instead of the unidentifiable remains, there were two largely intact bodies: one a man in his thirties, wearing Union Jack underwear; the other a woman.

Police were quickly able to find out how the blunder had been made—again, a simple transposition of numbers on the coffins. They knew who had been given the "wrong bodies." Inquiries were made through the FBI with the intention of telling the relatives of the mistake and restoring the bodies at Lockerbie to their families. However, police were horrified to find that the "wrong bodies" had already been cremated. In the end they decided just to send the two bodies they had to be cremated, swearing to secrecy all those who knew of the blunder.

The chief constable of the Dumfries and Galloway Constabulary has stated that after the internal investigation he could find no evidence that bodies had been mixed up. Scotland's Lord Advocate has also stated that investigations have found no basis in fact for a mixup of bodies.

10

THE INTELLIGENCE OPERATION

*"Gathering intelligence on these groups is one of the
most dangerous activities known to mankind."*

There is an unprecedented level of security and secrecy
surrounding the main thrust of the police investigation
into the Lockerbie bombing. The hunt is structured specifi-
cally to ensure that as few as possible of the people based
at the headquarters in Lockerbie Academy know the full
picture.

Although officers have been sent from Lockerbie to
West Germany, Finland, and the United States, they are
briefed only on the aspect of the inquiry that directly involves them. It is entirely likely that the only person with a
full overview of all the events surrounding Lockerbie is
Detective Chief Superintendent John Orr himself.

Information gathered by Western agencies is chan-
neled to Lockerbie through the British Secret Intelligence
Service, which is the only covert agency Orr has direct
dealings with, although CIA agents are regular visitors to
Lockerbie and the FBI have a team stationed in the Academy with a secure computer link back to Washington.

Dr. Bob Kupperman of the Institute of Strategic

Studies in Washington is an anti-terrorism advisor to the federal government. He says that while there is a clear determination at a political level of the U.S. administration to discover who bombed Flight 103, he can detect a reluctance among career officers to come up with answers.

His assertion is based on a knowledge of human nature. If a terrorist organization is found to have been responsible, and that organization has links to a particular country, then retaliatory action against that country is certain, which makes life difficult for career diplomats.

There are those who take a much harder view, saying that America at the highest levels lacks the will to retaliate, even if the identity of the bombers is confirmed more conclusively than with just intelligence reports.

Lt. Col. William Cowan is now a consultant—he used to be a member of the Intelligence Support Activity, a top-secret Pentagon unit. He says that from his experience, retaliation efforts get bogged down in bureaucratic bungling. In his opinion the U.S. government lacks political will for retaliation and also lacks experienced counter-terrorism experts working at a high level. "Retaliation involves a maze of agencies—the Navy, the Air Force, the Army, the Joint Chiefs of Staff, the Pentagon, the CIA— the National Security Council's decisions disappear into the bureaucracy."

Cowan says he was directly involved in an operation that identified those behind the bombing of a U.S. Marine base in Lebanon in 1983 that killed 243 people. They were able to furnish the Pentagon with a report detailing the names and addresses of the men directly involved in the bomb attack. Cowan suggested two options: assassination or arrest of those involved. "The report just disappeared," he says.

He now fears the same will happen in the case of the Pan Am bombers. American intelligence points at least part of the blame at Iran. Cowan says the Iranian Revolutionary Guards' base at Baalbeck in Lebanon would be a prime and obvious choice for a "hit." He says, "You can launch an attack with small, fast helicopter gunships while at the same time you put a unit of men on the ground. Or you could identify key people and put them under surveillance and carry out selective ambushes."

The problem is that the three main terrorist organizations with the capability and the motive to bomb Flight 103 are closely linked with Syria. Indeed Syria, a state that sponsors terrorism and even has it carried out by its own people, must be a suspect.

Because of the October 1988 discovery of the PFLP-GC personnel in West Germany and the equipment (already detailed) found on them, this group must be, and is, the main suspect for the atrocity. Dalkamoni, the Jordanian arrested by the BKA, is a key figure in Ahmad Jabril's organization, said by Western experts to number about five hundred adherents. Dalkamoni is thought to have spent a considerable amount of his time setting up PFLP-GC operations in Western Europe, including the Frankfurt ones.

The only real public pronouncement on the bombing has come from the PLO, which claims that Iran paid the PFLP-GC $10 million to carry out the attack. Because of the PLO's determination to negotiate a Palestinian homeland and the tentative moves that are being made, mainly by the Americans, to get the PLO and Israelis into a dialogue, the PLO has everything to gain by showing themselves to be a "responsible" organization that has turned its back on international terrorism. It would also suit Yasir Arafat to have his former lieutenant and now sworn enemy, Ahmad Jabril, fingered for the outrage.

Immediately, experts in terrorism spot holes in the PLO scenario. According to Paul Wilkinson of Aberdeen University, it would be unlikely that the PFLP-GC would act as paid mercenaries. He sees a similarity in objectives between them and the Iranian fundamentalists, but says that without detailed scrutiny of bank accounts used by Jabril, it would not be possible to reach a firm conclusion.

At Tel-Aviv University the world's leading expert on Palestinian terrorism, Dr. Ariel Merrari, says that Jabril is the most likely suspect for the bomb plot, but if Jabril was paid by the Iranians, it is the first time this has happened in the history of the organization.

Jabril is based in the Syrian capital of Damascus, with another camp across the border in a Syrian-controlled part of Lebanon, at Bar Elias. Dr. Merrari says that since its inception the PFLP-GC has relied exclusively on Syria for arms training and bases; in recent years it has also received money from Libya. At the same time, though, there are unconfirmed reports that Jabril was in the Iranian capital of Tehran prior to the Lockerbie bombing. "So I can't rule out that in some way Iran was an accomplice to the attack. Nevertheless, it is hard to imagine that Jabril would carry out a spectacular attack of this sort, an attack that has severe potential international implications, without receiving Syrian consent.

"The common objectives perceived between the Palestinian rejectionalists and the Iranian fundamentalists are a bit problematic. After the Rushdie affair and since this episode, we accept as a fact that there is a great deal of tension between Iran and the West. However, at the time of the attack at Lockerbie, it seems to me that Iran was not on the attack or that there was a worsening of relations with Western nations, but on the contrary, they seemed to be on the track of attracting Western goodwill and support."

That view is supported by the presence of an at-large West German industrial delegation in Tehran just before the Lockerbie bombing, investigating investment opportunities at the request of the Iranian government. But, like Professor Wilkinson, Dr. Merrari says that it is highly possible that hard-line factions in Iran would have acted contrary to the main thrust of the government.

If Jabril is responsible, says the doctor, Syrian complicity would be clear. Iranian links with any payment would be much harder to prove.

Jabril already has a track record of attacks on civilian aircraft, carried out in the same way suspected in the Lockerbie bombing. His agents in the past have duped innocent travelers into carrying onto aircraft bombs designed to explode in their luggage.

On 28 July 1971 an El Al flight from Rome to Tel Aviv was held up before departure when a suspect package was found in the luggage of a young Dutch girl. It proved to be a bomb. The girl had befriended a Palestinian in Rome, and he had given her the package, saying that it was a present for his family in Israel.

Two months later, on September 1, another dupe was recruited by Jabril to carry a bomb onto a flight from London to Tel Aviv. She was Yugoslavian and was again picked up by El Al security. She was questioned and released once it was established that she did not know what the "present" contained.

On 16 August 1972, El Al was not so lucky. In Rome two English girls carried on board a flight to Tel Aviv a record player that they had been given by two Palestinians for their family in Israel. The bomb inside exploded on board, but not completely, and the plane was able to land safely back in Rome. The two English girls were interrogated and the Palestinians arrested. However, the Italian authorities were not interested in drawing the wrath of Jabril, and so in February 1973 the two terrorists were released on bail and promptly fled Italy.

After the two attempts and the one successful bombing, airport-security services were overhauled to try and beat the bombers. They, in turn, responded by inventing more sophisticated devices.

The Toshiba BomBeat 453 found in Dalkamoni's car had two fuses linked to its detonator. The fuse that actually explodes such a bomb is a barometric one, designed to trigger when the plane reaches a certain altitude. Barometric fuses usually contain mercury, which expands as the nonpressurized cargo hold of a plane suffers a drop in atmospheric pressure as the aircraft climbs to its cruising height. In an effort to detect this type of device, most major airports have a decompression chamber; luggage is put into it and altitude decompression artificially reproduced. The result: the bomb triggers prematurely and only luggage is harmed.

To get past the decompression chamber, the PFLP-GC radio cassette recorder had a second fuse, a straight timing fuse, which would not activate the mercury fuse until sufficient time had elapsed to allow any bag containing the bomb to have completed its decompression tests and be loaded onto a plane. If such a bomb had been loaded onto Pan Am Flight 103 at Frankfurt, as Scottish detectives believe, the timing element of the fuse would have been longer than normal to ensure that the bomb went off after the luggage had been transferred in London and the plane was in flight to New York, rather than on the 727's first leg of the journey. In this way more people would be killed.

Devices like this are extremely difficult to construct to ensure, first, that they are not detected by airport security, and second, that they work. The skill needed to make a bomb like the one found on Dalkamoni is not widely available. Indeed, some terrorism experts believe that the construction of such a device would be beyond the capabilities of the PFLP-GC.

Raffie Eitan, Israel's former chief of military staff and now an anti-terrorism advisor to that government, is one such expert. He says that it is more than likely that if the PFLP-GC were responsible for actually getting the bomb on board, they did not construct it themselves. According to Eitan, the organization with the most sophisticated bomb-making techniques is the Arab Organization of 15 May (more commonly known as the May 15 Group) led by Abu Ibraheim.

This group was based in the Iraqi capital of Baghdad for many years before its leader was given a safe haven in Syria. Although it does not number many followers—perhaps thirty at most—they are at the forefront of terror techniques, thanks largely to the training given to Ibraheim by the Iraqis.

Raffie Eitan says: "Even if another organization was involved, [Ibraheim] has shown them his techniques. I've no doubt professionally about that. I base that on modus operandi, and up to this day I succeeded in these estimations of these things nine times out of ten."

Eitan says Jabril's attacks in the 1970s were all carried out in coordination with Ibraheim. In addition, during the past few years the May 15 Group has been further refining its bomb methods. "The Palestinian movements that are out of tune with Arafat's PLO all trade among themselves —technology, manpower, even budgets sometimes, and training and expertise. In my opinion, the PFLP-GC simply would not have the ability to make a device like the one at Lockerbie. They may have bought the device from Ibraheim, they may have traded for it, but the common cause between the groups would be sufficient to allow such transfers."

Eitan says it was a similar swapping of equipment that was behind the attempt on the El Al flight at Heathrow Airport in 1986. Nezar Hindawi duped his pregnant Irish girlfriend into carrying a device onto the plane, which was then spotted by that airline's security. Meanwhile, Hindawi promptly ran to the Syrian Embassy in London in an unsuccessful attempt to gain help.

According to the former Israeli chief of staff, the devices manufactured by Ibraheim can be small enough to fit into the lock of a suitcase. The PFLP-GC device had wafer-thin sheets of Semtex plastic explosive inserted between metal sheets made to resemble the radio cassette's transformer. It was activated by inserting a jack plug into the aerial socket.

Until recently, Jabril did not have an extensive cell structure in Western Europe. Several years ago eight members of his organization were found in London and expelled; two others were expelled from Sweden. The intelligence agencies that had been watching Dalkamoni as he traveled back and forth from Damascus to Frankfurt suspect that he was helping extend the network. Dr. Merrari says he is "an arch terrorist." According to the Tel Aviv University professor, it is impossible to say whether it was just coincidence that Jabril's men were in Frankfurt with the very type of device that blew up Flight 103. However, it is clear that they would not have been the only pro-Syrian terrorist groups in the area at that time working on this type of spectacular attack. Chillingly, Dr. Merrari says that further, similar outrages are almost certainly still being planned.

"On the other hand, it is by no means certain that Dalkamoni and his team were the only ones of Jabril's men in the field at the time. It is quite possible that although Dalkamoni and his team were caught, there was another Jabril team in Western Europe trying to achieve the same purpose."

In terms of world terror, Jabril is not the only one to have the ability and the motive to hit the U.S. in the dramatic fashion of Lockerbie.

Next in importance on the list is perhaps the best known of Middle Eastern terrorists, Abu Nidal. His group is, again, fundamentally opposed to Arafat and is known to operate a tight cell structure of terrorists in many European countries. His teams will often live in a country for many years before being activated.

Nidal's Damascus offices were closed down by the Syrian government after Western sanctions against that country were implemented in the wake of the Hindawi bomb attempt in 1986 on the El Al flight from London. However, most of his men are still based in Syria, with others in Syrian-controlled areas of Lebanon. Nidal himself is thought to have based himself in Libya. He is regarded as the world's most dangerous terrorist, held responsible for many of the world's most appalling acts of terrorism. He has, however, only one plane bombing to his "credit": an attack on a Gulf Air jet traveling from Abu Dhabi on 23 November 1983. The plane blew up in midair, killing 107 passengers and crew.

Also important enough for consideration are the Fatah Rebels, led by Abu Musa. Abu Musa's groups are also based in Damascus and Syrian-controlled Lebanon. He is held responsible for the attempted midair bombing of an El Al flight from Madrid in 1986, again using a courier who had been duped into carrying the device on board.

Gathering intelligence on these ruthless terrorist groups is one of the most dangerous activities on earth. In recent years the trend has been away from infiltration of organizations, intelligence agencies concentrating instead on electronic surveillance, satellite interception of communications, airport security, and simple monitoring of movements of key personnel in the organizations under scrutiny. Intelligence experts say that as a result of these activities, a great many attempted outrages are averted and the entire operation is kept secret to protect the sources of the tip-off, whether they be human or electronic.

However, Dr. Merrari believes that nowadays there is not enough human infiltration of terrorist groups. "In fighting terrorism, the human element is very important—intelligence gathered by agents. Unfortunately, Western intelligence agencies are relying more and more on electronic gadgets, rather than human agents."

Former CIA agent Miles Copeland says that the old CIA method of protecting sources was to build up a profile of a bogus source to divert attention away from your agent in the field. While this is relatively easy in some circumstances, it is far more difficult in the world of the terrorist.

Copeland uses as an example a spy in the Kremlin with a piece of "hot information" on which action would have to be taken. "When the Soviets see us acting, they are going to say 'Ah-ha, they've got intelligence on us,' and they'll try and find where the leak is.

"That means the poor little guy who let the information out is sitting quaking in his boots. One day the KGB barge in. He sees the guys in dark suits heading toward his desk and thinks, 'My God, they've caught me.' And the KGB go right by him and cart off the guy at the next desk, some poor little innocent guy."

Copeland says this goes on the world over. When a security service gets a tip-off that a plane or an airport or whatever is to be hit, they have to handle that information in such a way as to make the perpetrator think that it came from somewhere else.

These would undoubtedly have been the tactics used by Mossad, the Israeli security agency, when, two months before Lockerbie, it tipped off the West about a possible attack on an aircraft from Frankfurt. It is thought that this tip led, in turn, to the CIA tipping off the West Germans and the consequent arrest of Dalkamoni.

Copeland says that while he does not know intimate details of the Lockerbie investigation, he does know it is going very well. "They've gotten commendations for this. One of the first things President Bush did after getting in office was to go out to Langley [CIA headquarters in Virginia] and make a talk to the CIA people there, saying what a marvelous job they've done and how terrorism has been buttoned up.

"After the Libya raid, for example, you had all these politicians saying, 'Well, the Libya raid worked because it stopped terrorism.' It didn't work at all. The number of terrorism attempts in the months right after quadrupled. Kids in the refugee camps were lining up, volunteering to go on suicide missions.

"The reasons why there were not any successful terrorist attempts after that was that they intensified operations of all the intelligence services to nip these things in the bud before they started."

The weak point of any competent terrorist organization is the number of people who have to be used to mount their attacks. The Lockerbie bomb was made in such a sophisticated manner so the bombers could beat the airport security systems. But there had to be a workshop somewhere capable of making it. It had to be tested. It had to be placed on the aircraft by one of only two routes: either carried on by a passenger, for some reason; or placed on it by people gaining access to the airside of an airport, people who should not be there.

The job for the intelligence agents is to get some sort of penetration into the group. Copeland sums it up like this: "If you wanted a spy in the British Foreign Office, the best person to approach is not the minister or the senior civil servants. It's a secretary or someone in the file room, some lowly clerk who handles the secret information, provided it's written down.

"The problem is, with terrorists, their organization is pretty primitive. Not the operational side, but they don't keep records like we do, so you have to have guys that take this into account."

New laws in the United States make Lockerbie the first international terrorist inquiry of any size that has directly involved the FBI operating overseas. Traditionally they have been a domestic investigation body, but the increase in drug trafficking and terrorism led the federal authorities to give them some jurisdiction overseas.

State Department sources and State Department agents (who make up the third force of U.S. intelligence operations, after the CIA), are highly critical of the work the FBI has done on Lockerbie to date. They say the Bureau's reports so far have resembled school essays rather than any credible attempts at investigation, though how much credence to put on the opinions expressed during such nonattributable briefings is hard to assess, considering the turf wars that are traditional between U.S. intelligence arms.

The "routine" police work—starting on the ground in Lockerbie and then stretching out, eventually, possibly all over the world—and the intelligence-gathering operation, have to meet in the middle at some time.

The organizations and countries behind Lockerbie were made known in general terms to the investigators by intelligence sources before it was publicly confirmed that a bomb had brought down Flight 103. Within hours of the explosion police and press alike took particular interest in the only Arab on the plane, Khaled Jafaar, a twenty-one-year-old naturalized American citizen whose family come from Baalbeck in Lebanon. It has been persistently speculated in the press that Jafaar, one way or another, carried the bomb on board.

The student had been visiting his grandfather in Baalbeck, and on his way home for Christmas in Detroit (where his father, Nadir Jafaar, now runs a gas station), he stayed with childhood friends, now refugees, in Frankfurt. Baalbeck, in Syrian-controlled Lebanon, is base to a number of terrorists and not far from the PFLP-GC's Lebanese camp at Bar Elias. There is a convincing circumstantial case against Jafaar as, at the very least, an unwitting accomplice to the Lockerbie bombing.

However, investigators believe that at least three women on the flight had Lebanese or Palestinian boyfriends, which makes them prime suspects for carrying on the bomb (see Chapter 13).

In late March 1989 the part of the investigation based in the United States began to get bogged down in conflicts among the various investigating bodies. State Department anti-terrorism experts gave off-the-record briefings to selected Washington journalists on the progress of the inquiries and, more important for them, on how the FBI was bungling it. The Bureau, on the other hand, was acutely aware that its new overseas jurisdiction was being given its first main test with the Lockerbie investigation.

Slowly, the FBI began hitting back. Determined to show that it was getting on with the job, it too gave off-the-record briefings to selected journalists. On 11 April 1989 reporters at CBS were briefed by the FBI—as a final attempt, it is thought—to bury the slurs of incompetence made by the Bureau's fellow investigators. That briefing culminated in a report on CBS the following day saying that the exact identity of the Lockerbie bomber was known to the FBI and that a major development—an arrest was hinted—was likely within eight days. CBS reported that the man who had placed the bomb on the plane was a relative of Dalkamoni and was a member of the PFLP-GC.

In Scotland the various matches between U.S. investigators were watched with a mixture of annoyance and amusement. The British inquiry had been water-tight. Nothing had leaked and it was feared that the FBI leaks could set back their own investigation by weeks. In an unusual reaction to the CBS report, Scotland's Lord Advocate issued a statement saying that while he did not wish to comment on the CBS report, he would admit to a "narrowing in the focus" of the police inquiry.

A senior officer in the Scottish investigation says that when the CBS report came out, it obviously had its origins in the FBI. The Scottish authorities kept quiet because they did not want to start a transatlantic row that could well have led to further off-the-record briefings and to further (and perhaps irreparable) damage being done to the inquiry.

The determination of Detective Superintendent John Orr to get what he might call "a result" from his mammoth investigation cannot be doubted. The confidence of the U.S. relatives of the victims of Flight 103 in the determination of politicians is less well founded.

Bert Ammerman, chairman of the relatives' political committee, says: "I believe that within seventy-two hours of the bombing, our intelligence sources knew who did it and what country supported it—Iran.

"That has given our executive and State Department a tough problem because, if a government is actively involved, it is no longer terrorism. The term they like to use is 'state-sponsored terrorism' because they don't want to call it what it is: an act of war against the United States by another country."

When this history-teacher-turned-politician is asked if he believes whether this complication would actually lead to a reluctance by governments to establish blame for the bombing of Flight 103, Bert Ammerman gives a wry smile and says: "That is a very, very crucial statement. A very critical part of this whole thing. It would seem that there is not as strong a commitment as possible to identify every part of this because of the repercussions.

"If they do identify Iran or Libya as actually supporting this—and I think it will be Iran—there will be a huge outcry for an appropriate reaction from our government to show that we will not tolerate this. I don't know if certain officials in our government are ready to accept what might have to take place. This way, if they don't find out what has taken place, they'll not have to do it.

"I cynically imagine that some leaders in West Germany, Britain, and the United States privately said to each other: 'These goddamn terrorists, these Iranians, they can't do anything right. Why couldn't this plane have blown up over the Atlantic and then we wouldn't have had this?' But it didn't. It happened over the land, and now they have the evidence."

Ammerman says that the main concern of the Victims of Flight 103 Group is to ensure that the issue never goes away until it is properly resolved.

On 3 April 1989 the relatives held a vigil outside the White House, 103 days after the downing of Flight 103. Afterward, Ammerman and three others were ushered inside for a private meeting with President George Bush. Bush told the relatives that he was determined to identify the bombers and take appropriate action against them and any countries that may have been involved.

Therefore, if the PFLP-GC is designated the perpetrator, action against it will be taken when the investigation has come up with concrete answers. The PFLP-GC is vulnerable to attack. On 20 March 1989 Israeli jets strafed Jabril's camp in Bar Elias, in the Beka'a valley in Lebanon, six miles west of the border with Syria. Fifteen people—civilians as well as members of the PFLP-GC—were killed in the attack on a vehicle repair shop and a single-story office building. At the time Israeli Defense Minister Yitzhak Rabin said: "I believe that those who deserved to get it, got it." The reason for the raid was not given, but it was speculated that the Israeli government may have taken into account the growing suspicion of PFLP-GC complicity in Lockerbie.

An attack such as this can be fairly simple and effective. However, if Jabril's visit to the Iranian Revolutionary Guards last year is taken as evidence of Iranian complicity, as well as the fact that he does nothing without the approval of the Syrian government, the concept of retaliation becomes much more difficult. Syria is a key player in the difficult politics of the Middle East, having control over a substantial part of Lebanon. President al-Assad also has very close links with the Soviet Union, which, despite Mr. Gorbachev, may take very unkindly to one of its primary Middle Eastern allies coming under direct American attack.

These are main reasons why the families and others fear the lack of political determination to thoroughly identify the real men behind Lockerbie.

It is a fear that has a compelling logic. Dr. Ariel Merrari says that if, indeed, the track leads to Syria, the United States, Britain, and West Germany would be in a great dilemma.

"Retaliating against Syria is not retaliating against Libya, for instance. Syria is a much tougher nut, it's much more dangerous also, because Syria is closer to the Soviet Union, and military retaliation against Syria may be very, very dangerous.

"I cannot predict what the Western countries involved would do if the track does lead to Syria. I would just say that the longer the length of time before they reveal the Syrian connection, the lesser the likelihood that military retaliation may be taken.

"Logically, you would think there would be a reluctance on behalf of governments to come up with an answer, but I cannot say this contention is supported by my official friends in America, Germany, and Britain. They all claim that they do invest a great effort into finding out who was behind the Lockerbie attack. The Americans claim publicly it is the largest-ever manhunt into terrorism, and I was told the same privately by knowledgeable American officials.

"I don't know what to say. Logically, they should be dragging their feet on purpose, but I have no evidence to support this logic."

The reason why the Scottish police believe that the FBI hampered their inquiry is that the briefing given by the Bureau to CBS was accurate.

Someone within the PFLP-GC structure appears to have been talking. The West Germans say Dalkamoni and his assistant Ghadanfar have said very little, but it is clear that someone in the terror organization has given investigators more than just a clue. Since March 1989 police interest in the PFLP-GC has focused on one individual— Dalkamoni's younger brother, Abdul Fatteh Dalkamoni. Detectives believe that he is the one who tricked a passenger on Flight 103 into carrying the bomb.

Dr. Merrari places the elder Dalkamoni high up in the structure of the PFLP-GC. His younger brother has no terrorist convictions on record and far less is known about him. Abdul Dalkamoni is, however, known to have been involved with his elder brother in the establishment of the PFLP-GC cell in Frankfurt. He was then to have played a role directly connected with the operations planned for that cell.

The West German authorities will not confirm that the younger Dalkamoni was among the fourteen Palestinians detained in the October raids, but other sources say that he was, and that he was then allowed to go free. Whether it was simply for lack of evidence, or because the BKA intended to keep him under surveillance in the hope of being led to further arrests, may never be known.

Detectives believe that the younger Dalkamoni is probably now safe in the PFLP-GC's hands in one of their bases in Syria or Lebanon, and at the moment out of reach. However, before the FBI gave the off-the-record briefing to CBS, it had been hoped that he could be picked up on a foray into the West.

While airports all over the world are on the lookout for Dalkamoni the younger, the BKA's investigations into the PFLP-GC have shown that that organization is still functioning in West Germany. Over the weekend of 16/17 April 1989, the BKA staged another raid in Neuss, in an apartment occupied by a Palestinian suspected of being a member of the PFLP-GC. Two stereo rack-system radio tuners and one television monitor were found and taken to BKA headquarters in Wiesbaden. As two explosives experts began examining the first of the radio tuners, it blew up, killing one of the men outright and seriously injuring his colleague. The second radio tuner and the television were later defused with a robot.

A spokesman for the West German Attorney General says that despite their suspicion of the apartment's occupant's involvement in the PFLP-GC, they had no proof against him and so he was freed after questioning. A BKA spokesman says that their inquiry is still very active, and they are refusing to give any details. They would not even have made public the raid in Neuss had it not been for the fatal consequences.

One thing is certain. If one of those devices was planned for use against an aircraft, there would have been another Lockerbie disaster.

11

THE WARNINGS

"Warnings and threats . . . are all too common in the
civil aviation industry."

If airline security is designed to stop bombs being put on
aircrafts, then the Pan Am security was flawed on December twenty-first.

At airports worldwide, individual airlines (or their
agents) are responsible for the security of each of their
flights. The rule is that the airport will provide a basic
level of security and it is up to the airline to accept or
improve on it as they think fit.

Police believe that the cassette recorder containing
the bomb was placed on Flight 103 at Frankfurt. Pan Am
will not discuss the level of security applied to that flight
because of impending litigation instigated by the relatives
of those who died. However, it is possible to paint an
accurate scenario of the security that would have been in
force at Frankfurt prior to the departure of the first part of
the Flight 103—the 727 that left Frankfurt at four-fifty
P.M. local time.

Security for the flight would have been the responsibility of Pan Am's wholly owned security company, Alert
Management Systems Inc., based in Florida. Security at
Frankfurt Airport itself is always maintained at a relatively

high state of alert; the West German authorities say it does not alter from week to week, as some international airports do, responding to the air security bulletins that are current at any given time.

Security is expensive. If baggage is X-rayed, the cost of each item put through the machine has to be borne by the airline. It is also time consuming. If thorough checks were carried out on every passenger and every item of baggage, the air transport system would grind to a halt.

To cut down on cost and delay, Pan Am at Frankfurt that afternoon, in common with other carriers, would in all likelihood have been employing what is known as profile screening. That means trying to spot potential hijackers or bomb carriers with routine and basic checks. The idea behind the technique is to identify those who are clearly not "international terrorists," and subject those who may be to a higher degree of checking.

In practice, this is often left to one single check: the passport. If a passenger is carrying a passport of a country that does not harbor or sponsor terrorism, that should be sufficient to ensure that he or she is not picked out for detailed searching. It would have been Pan Am's practice at Frankfurt to assume that anyone carrying a U.K., U.S., or West German passport would not be a threat. (In their response to my 22 March 1989 letter, however, Pan Am says it was not their practice to X-ray only the luggage of non-American, West German, and United Kingdom nationals starting their journey in London. See page 233.)

Profiling can be more refined, and it should be, but the constraints of time mean that it is usually overlooked. Simple questions can be asked to give further clues—for example, "Did you pack this luggage yourself?" Then the tickets can give vital information. A terrorist is likely to have bought a ticket at the last minute and to have bought it with cash so that he or she couldn't be traced through a credit card.

Only one airline—El Al, the Israeli national carrier— maintains a thorough and permanent high level of security. It is nearly impossible to achieve a foolproof system that will beat the terrorist on every occasion, and El Al has been successfully attacked on a number of times. However, a great number of terrorist bids have been thwarted by their security.

Former British Airways security chief Dennis Phipps says that the problem of airport security is twofold. First, the entire worldwide airport system is creaking under the strain of many more passengers than individual facilities were designed to cope with. Second, in the commercial world, security is often regarded as a necessary evil, an expense with little visible return. Phipps is particularly scornful of the practice of some airlines to hire outside security services, oftentimes employing the cheapest contractor, who, in turn, employs the cheapest available staff. This means a low caliber of personnel at the front line of the fight against the sophisticated terrorist.

El Al security is two-pronged. All luggage is hand searched by staff, and passengers are asked a series of profiling questions. Not only are the answers to those questions important, but also the appearance and manner of the passenger. El Al officials are highly trained to look for telltale signs of stress and nervousness that may indicate a terrorist at the check-in desk. The result of this thoroughness is that El Al passengers have to check in three hours before takeoff, which other airlines see as a major bar to attracting customers.

El Al maintains its security at this level on all routes at all times. It is neither increased nor decreased to match prevailing international tensions. Most other airlines and airports tend to alter their security from time to time in accordance with security bulletins issued by government departments and designed to advise carriers of specific threats. Pan Am, as an American carrier, would mainly rely on threat information from the U.S. Federal Aviation Administration, but in addition would receive security bulletins prepared by the countries from which it operates.

How these security bulletins are compiled and the intelligence assessed is a closely guarded secret in all Western countries. This is mainly to protect the sources of those intelligence reports.

Ex-CIA man Miles Copeland says that if security bulletins were widely available, sources will dry up. This is because terrorist groups have people working in the international air-travel system, and they would report back to their masters any increased security measures designed to counter some perceived threat, thereby tipping off the plotters that their plan had been uncovered and helping them to look for the source of that leak. Copeland goes so far as to say that agents' lives are put at risk by bulletins becoming public.

In the United States, assessment is done by a committee of intelligence personnel drawn from the FAA, the CIA, the FBI, and the Defense Intelligence Agency. In Britain, the Department of Transport takes the lead in threat assessment, using information supplied to it by the British SIS and the FAA, as well as similar bodies in other countries.

The anonymous call to the U.S. Embassy in Helsinki made on December 5 was, according to the Finnish security police, dismissed almost immediately. However, there are, as we have seen, many inconsistencies in the subsequent handling of the threat.

The other relevant series of warning bulletins were those relating to the 26 October 1988 raids in Frankfurt and the arrest of Dalkamoni on the outskirts of Neuss.

The BKA in West Germany flashed a warning of what had been uncovered in the raids to Interpol in Paris within twenty-four hours of the arrest. A spokesman says that on November 1 they called a press conference at BKA headquarters in Frankfurt to show the guns, ammunition, and bomb.

Then it was decided to invite what are known as the Trevi States—the signatories to the international terrorist convention—to Frankfurt on November 15 to give intelligence experts a detailed rundown on exactly what had been found on the PFLP-GC members. Participants at this meeting were given photographs of the cassette-recorder bomb to take away with them.

British experts were at the meeting, and by November 22 they had constructed a model of the BomBeat 453 and security staff at Heathrow were practicing detecting it in luggage.

The first two FAA bulletins after the October raids made no mention of the barometric bomb that had been found in the possession of the PFLP-GC. The first details

of the device came in Bulletin 88 19, dated November 17
—three weeks after the arrests.

> Preliminary analysis by West German authorities of
> improvised explosive devices (IED's) found in vari-
> ous stages of preparation during the recent arrests of
> members of the PFLP-GC in West Germany dis-
> closed one IED consisting of a Toshiba BomBeat 453
> radio containing approximately 300 grams of a
> plastic-type explosive wrapped in a metallic-coated
> "Tobler" brand candy wrapper. The IED contained
> an electrical detonator . . . [At this point, the bul-
> letin gives detailed construction advice.] . . . The
> IED contained a barometric device connected to a
> computer chip (NFI) which was believed functional
> and apparently part of the trigger or arming func-
> tion. The potential target of this IED cannot be
> identified at this time, although it was determined
> that IED would be very difficult to detect via normal
> X-ray inspection, indicating that it might be in-
> tended to pass undisclosed through areas subject to
> extensive security controls such as airports.

The usual FAA comment is appended to the end of the
bulletin.

> On October 26, 1988, West German police detained
> 16 persons from various cities throughout West Ger-
> many for suspicion of involvement with planned ter-
> rorist actions by the PFLP-GC. Of the 16 detained,
> 14 were Palestinians. Twelve were eventually re-

leased and four remain in custody. Ammunition, explosives, and numerous weapons were seized, as well
as items indicating the manufacture of bombs and
other IED's. Also seized were false passports and
identity documents from [a list of five nations de-
leted for security reasons] . . . The PFLP-GC was
founded in 1968 by Ahmad Jabril [American spell-
ing] as a splinter of the PFLP led by George Hab-
bash. The PFLP-GC has been characterized as an
essentially military organization consisting of ap-
proximately 500 members and concentrating on attacks against Israeli targets within Israel and the
occupied territories, such as hang-glider and hot-air-
balloon attacks into Israel. The group has not been
known to undertake terrorist attacks in Europe, and
the arrest of this number of operatives and weap-
onry outside of the Middle East is significant.

Again, the FAA authorized the bulletin information to be
disseminated to embassies.

The bulletin was late in being issued, and incorrect.
In the U.S. Defense Department's official profile of terrorist organizations, the PFLP-GC is credited with two European hijackings, and a machine-gun attack on an El Al
flight from Zurich.

In addition, the documents record Ahmad Jabril as
saying at a press conference in Libya in 1986: "There will
be no safety for any traveler on an Israeli or U.S. airliner."

The earlier FAA bulletins—88 17 and 88 18, which
were written on November 2 and 3—mention the
PFLP-GC raids, in the first, and then the arrests, in the

second, as some of the "many terrorist-related events of concern."

Bulletin 88 17 says there is no information on specific targets that would be attacked by any of the numerous terrorist groups involved. The situation, says the bulletin, is volatile. Under "Action required," the bulletin suggests that airline security personnel "disseminate the information to corporate officials able to take precautionary measures in the event that specific threat information is developed that must be passed and reacted to extremely quickly."

Bulletin 88 18 focuses on the possibility of a hijacking in the first half of November, again linking the warning with the PFLP-GC raid and apparently failing to notice that the radio cassette recorder was designed to blow up a plane. Bombing was not mentioned in that warning as a possible or probable alternative course of terrorist action.

On December 5 came bulletin 88 20, which warned that the use of "improvised explosive devices" (IED's) remained a favored method of attack. But the FAA restricted its advice to telling airlines to stick rigorously to existing security measures.

Then, on December 7, the FAA warned airlines that on two occasions phony law-enforcement officers had made inquiries at TWA in Frankfurt Airport about procedures for transporting pistols, explosives, and a detonator. No attempt was made to detain or question the bogus police officers.

So by Wednesday, December 21, Pan Am had every reason to be extremely vigilant as the 109 passengers were checked for Flight 103 to London's Heathrow and New

York's Kennedy airports. The airline knew that the PFLP-GC was operating in West Germany. It knew that the Toshiba BomBeat 453 radio cassette recorder had been adapted to be a hard-to-detect lethal bomb, and it "knew" from the Helsinki warning, still in force, that a passenger might be duped into carrying a bomb onto a flight from Frankfurt to the United States. Although that warning to the Helsinki embassy is now regarded as a hoax, the FAA did not rescind it officially until December 21.

At four-fifty P.M. Flight 103 took off from Frankfurt carrying the 109 passengers, one of whom may have been tricked into carrying onto the aircraft a radio cassette recorder outfitted with a deadly bomb.

When the 727 landed an hour and ten minutes later at Pier 7 at Heathrow, the luggage for the forty-nine passengers checked through to New York and Detroit was manhandled out of the hold of the 727 and placed in the forward cargo hold of the 747 clipper *Maid of the Seas,* parked at the next pier—*without further checks being made.*

The day after the crash, U.S. State Department officials made inquiries concerning the security precautions in force at Frankfurt the night before the fatal flight 103. They reported back as a matter of urgency:

The following procedures have been in force for over a year:

All passengers' hand luggage is physically searched. Tickets and passports are checked, and passengers are questioned as to whether they packed their bags and maintained custody over them.

Non-American and non-German passengers are subjected to the FAA profile, and, if they "fit," all their luggage is physically searched.

After check-in, German security examines all hand-carried luggage and passengers pass through a magnetometer.

Passengers who fit the profile are carefully rechecked at the departure gate.

Embassy team verified that state security advisories and FAA security bulletins have been promptly passed to airport and airline officials.

Since the report to Pan Am on December 7, 1988, regarding the threat received from Helsinki, Pan Am Frankfurt instituted an additional lookout for profile suspects. This course of action is still in effect. In addition to checks for non-Americans/Germans outlined, any profile suspects' hold baggage is subjected to an X-ray check subsequent to check-in.

Security officials confirmed that they were aware of the recent seizure of a bomb with a barometric switch in Frankfurt and were especially concerned about such devices since they are very difficult to detect.

So again it can be seen that unless a passenger fits the profile, only the most elementary of checks were made.

In fact, if the bomb carrier were a U.S. or German citizen (and it is thought that U.K. passport holders were also in this category), his check-through luggage would not be X-rayed. In Jabril's three previous midair bombing attempts, and in his one successful one, innocent passengers had been duped into carrying the bombs.

In Washington, D.C., the House of Representatives Transportation subcommittee, under Chicago congress-woman Cardis Collins, had made a thorough investigation into the warning bulletins from the FAA. The subcommittee notes that it took the FAA three weeks to alert U.S. air carriers (and the U.K. Department of Transport) that a terrorist group in West Germany had constructed at least one bomb designed to evade normal detection procedures and blow up an aircraft. They go on to say the West Germans similarly wasted two weeks before sending this vital information to U.S. airlines, along with a photograph of the Toshiba radio cassette player.

In the House of Commons on 21 March 1989, Transport Secretary Paul Channon gave his most detailed account to date of the warnings issued on the radio cassette bomb by his own department. He said that the first the department had learned of the October 26 raids was on November 17. The next day the department received a copy of an FAA bulletin, but he declined to say which one—whether it was one of the first two (bulletins 88 17 and 18), which omitted mention of the radio cassette bomb, or bulletin 88 19, which did describe it.

Then he said: "Having received further information on November twenty-second about the radio cassette bomb, the department issued a warning by telex on the same day to United Kingdom airports and airlines, pointing to the possible existence of other such devices. On the basis of this, the authorities at Heathrow Airport simulated a radio bomb and distributed photographs for the training of their security staff."

Channon went on to say that his department subsequently sought photographs of the West German radio bomb and additional information. A supplementary circular was prepared and signed by the department's principal security officer on December 19 but it was not sent out because they were still waiting for color photographs of the bomb. Details of the bomb that blew up Pan Am 103 were eventually sent through normal channels to Pan Am and other airlines and airports in the second week of January.

On 21 December 1988, as 243 passengers were milling around the departure lounge waiting for Flight 103 to be called, their luggage was being loaded into the hold of the *Maid of the Seas.* One of the transfer bags from Frankfurt was examined.

If normal procedures were being followed, only a very few items of luggage of passengers starting their flight at Heathrow would have been checked by X ray. If the Heathrow passengers passed the profile test employed at the airport, their hold luggage would not have been X-rayed. That means that none of the U.S. or British passport holders would have had his or her luggage X-rayed.

The stable door was belatedly bolted by the British Department of Transport. On December 28, the day it was confirmed that a bomb had been the cause of the Lockerbie disaster, the DOT issued a new directive to American airlines.

The operator shall not cause or permit any baggage
which is being transferred directly from another
flight to be placed in the hold of his aircraft unless
that baggage has been searched by hand or screened
by X ray, and when there is doubt as to its contents,
searched by hand to a sufficient standard to ensure
that it does not contain any weapons or components
thereof, explosives, or any components of any explosive device.

In the immediate aftermath of the disaster, the National
Aviation Security Committee, a DOT body, prepared a
confidential report on the handling of Flight 103. Point 7
of that report confirmed:

Hold baggage belonging to passengers transferring
from the Boeing 727 aircraft from Frankfurt to the
Boeing 747 aircraft was transferred directly without
being screened: pieces were moved separately from
the Boeing 727 baggage container to the Boeing 747
baggage container.

If the new DOT regulation of December 28 had been in
force one week earlier, then there would have at least been
a chance of Heathrow staff picking up the radio cassette
bomb missed by Frankfurt.

In 1986 Pan Am became worried about its security and
commissioned a report into their procedures from a New
York–based consultancy firm, KPI Inc., acknowledged to
be world experts in their field.

KPI's final 200-page report, given to the Pan Am board, concluded: "Pan Am is highly vulnerable to most forms of terrorist attack. The fact that no major disaster has occurred to date is merely providential."

KPI told Pan Am in that report that they were wrong to take citizenship as a security classifier: "As a rule, American citizens and citizens of the host country are considered 'safer' as regards their belly baggage, which is not checked in any way." Pan Am had "an over-reliance on technical appliances [X-ray machines] which inherently cannot serve today as instrumental aids, and inadequate efforts to mark out suspects."

KPI said that Pan Am had made no real attempt to test procedures. They also pointed to vital flaws in profiling techniques and their application:

No effort was found at most airports to mark out a passenger or suspect according to profile criteria, and accordingly to subject him to special questioning or searching . . . In cases where baggage is checked by X-raying, even an experienced and watchful security officer cannot see and identify a weapon or explosive charge, and the right course of action is to open the baggage and search it manually. Yet from many baggage items we saw being X-rayed, almost none was opened and hand searched. Out of the prescribed six departure questions, passengers are usually asked few, if any. From the way the questions are put, it is clear that the questioners do not understand the importance of the questions, nor do the passengers. Thus, remarkably, at most stations

there had not been for weeks even one passenger
who was delivering a gift. Our experience is that, by
asking these questions in a proper way, one gets
completely different and much better responses.

KPI then delivered a devastating indictment: "In conclusion, there are no adequate safeguards under the presently
operating security system that would prevent a passenger
from boarding a plane with explosives on his person,
whether or not he is aware of the fact."

Congresswoman Collins' subcommittee was assured
by Pan Am that the security breaches in the report had
been addressed. The subcommittee comments: ". . . the
bombing of Pan Am Flight 103 suggest[s] otherwise, as
does information which the subcommittee has obtained
from a variety of sources concerning the recent and current status of Pan Am security."

After Pan Am increased ticket prices in 1986 with the
security supplement, the corporation advertised the five-
dollar fact to try and counter the American public's
prevailing fear of transatlantic flying, brought about by
worries of reprisals following the Tripoli bombing raid.
Full-page advertisements in U.S. magazines and newspapers made great claims as to the lengths Pan Am went in
order to maintain security at a high level.

However, KPI warned the corporation in its report:

The striking discordance between the actual security
level and the security as advertised by the corporation may sooner or later become a cause of harmful
publicity. In the event of casualties or damage result-

ing from terrorist action, the question of fraudulent advertisement would assume even greater significance.

The investigation by the House of Representatives Transportation subcommittee is the only real public probe into the Flight 103 story in either Britain or the United States. Pan Am has only grudgingly cooperated with the subcommittee. In addition its work has been badly disrupted by a bizarre series of events that led to the sacking of its main Pan Am Flight 103 investigator and her boss.

Sheila Hershow spent sixteen years covering Capitol Hill in Washington as a TV reporter before joining the staff of the subcommittee. Her determination to uncover the truth behind the bombing of Flight 103 resulted in the public finally hearing the story of the warnings that went apparently unheeded, and the inadequacies of airline security in general and Pan Am's in particular.

On 23 March 1989 Hershow's boss, John Galloway, walked into her office in room B350 of the Rayburn Office Building, which houses the private offices of members of the House of Representatives. Taking her filing-cabinet key from her, he sent her home without explanation.

Despite numerous attempts to contact subcommittee chairman Cardis Collins, Hershow could get no reason for her suspension. Eventually the Chicago congresswoman did return one of Hershow's calls and said that the matter would be cleared up on her return to Washington. It was —on 6 April 1989 Hershow was fired. She refuses to talk about her sacking, but colleagues in her office circulated a confidential memo that Galloway had written to Collins,

describing Hershow as "so uncontrollable and so dangerous that I would recommend that she be dismissed, re-
gardless of the consequences to the Pan Am investigation."

Five out of six of her colleagues on the inquiry team
have supported Hershow. The day after her dismissal,
Galloway was also fired by Congresswoman Collins.

It is understood that at the time of her firing, Hershow was uncovering evidence that directly contradicts
the public pronouncements of the U.S. State Department
over the Helsinki warning. Hershow had found documen-
tary proof that the warning had not been considered a
hoax by the State Department until after December 21.
Despite this, Hershow's colleagues do not support any attempt to put the firings down to a conspiracy theory. They
say they believe that the roots of her dismissal lie purely in
interoffice politics.

However, the relatives of victims of Flight 103 were
disappointed by her dismissal.

12

AIR SECURITY

"Willful misconduct."

It is quite likely that the notices on the canteen wall in the U.S. Embassy in Moscow detailing the "Helsinki warning" tipped off State Department employees to choose an alternate carrier for flights to the United States.

The questions that relatives of those who died aboard Flight 103 ask incessantly are: Why should the government look after its own? Why should their staff have been told of the threat and not our loved ones?

Pan Am says that Flight 103 was only two thirds full simply because it was the last flight of the day and, as such, would not normally be expected to be full. This does not square with reality. The six o'clock flight to New York was popular with business executives. It allowed them a full day in London, and then, taking into account the time difference, to be home in the New York suburbs in time for a reasonably full night's sleep.

Congressional sources say that there is clear evidence the Helsinki warning and its subsequent partial publication did have a profound effect on bookings on Pan Am flights from Frankfurt to the United States. Indeed, copies of cables have come into the hands of congressional investigators in which Pan Am officials in New York clearly try to establish the precise cost of the cancellations and lost revenue.

The State Department has said that it was a breach of normal procedures for the warning to be displayed so prominently in Moscow; they should have been in the possession only of the post's security officer. But as a State Department official admitted: "What sort of security officer is not going to phone his wife and say, 'Take the kids off the flight,' or phone his buddies and pass on the warning to them?"

So it would seem that the only real positive result of the warnings issued by the FAA was to prevent a number of government employees losing their lives on Flight 103.

The coauthor of the KPI, Inc. report is Isaac Yeffet, a former security chief for El Al and now based in New York. He is scathing of airline security, particularly that of the U.S. carriers. He says that it would be unfair to single out Pan Am. They were simply unlucky; their security is no better and no worse than that of other airlines.

Yeffet reinforces the point made in the 1986 report about overreliance on technical equipment to detect the terrorist: "I am completely against the idea that X ray can give you the answer to good security. You cannot identify Semtex through an X-ray machine. What you see is dark colors. Now, if you carry a radio, you can conceal Semtex and no one will see it. A professional and alert security officer may manage to spot something unusual and have it checked. However, at all airports I have been at, they hire the lowest level of the private security company in order to save money.

"The priority of the security is so low that, if they did

not have to follow the FAA regulations, they might say, 'We don't want security at all.' They may well say, 'We are commercial airlines. We are not sponsored by the government. We are looking to make money.'"

Yeffet says in his quiet, measured tones, that while airlines must, by law, impose certain security arrangements, they look for the cheapest ways to do it. He says this applies to nearly all airlines. "No matter how many warnings have gone out, it all comes down to one man sitting looking at an X-ray machine, and if he's not very good . . ."

Yeffet says FAA regulations in the United States require every piece of luggage on an international flight to be X-rayed. During a recent check on security at U.S. airports, Yeffet came across a prime example of what he says is the problem in aviation security. He questioned closely an X-ray machine operator at the Denver, Colorado airport, who was checking luggage for an international flight.

"He had been given only eight hours' training before he became in charge of this X-ray machine. He said he remembers from what he was told that he has to look at the monitor for the green colors, that mean for him that it might be metal in the luggage. When we asked him, 'What about dark pictures that you see on nearly every piece of luggage?' he said it might be books. We decided to put pressure on him and said, 'Let's say it's not books. It might be something more suspicious than books.' His answer was, 'I was instructed to ask the passenger what he has inside his luggage. Whatever the passenger tells me, I have to trust him, to leave him, and send his luggage to the aircraft.'"

On that basis, Yeffet says, why do we need security at all? The Warsaw Convention of 1929 limits the liability of airlines in cases of crashes to a maximum payout of $75,000. The Convention was designed to "protect fledgling airlines" from compensation claims that would bankrupt them, at a time when aircraft safety was not what it has to be today. Only if an airline can be found guilty of "willful misconduct" that has led to a crash can that payout ceiling be exceeded.

Pan Am is now facing a welter of litigation from relatives of those who died in the air and on the ground, as well as from people in Lockerbie who were injured in the crash.

John and Janet Smith, badly burned when their home at 17 Sherwood Crescent burst into flames following the crash of the wings and fuel a couple of doors away, have filed cases in the United States against Pan Am and its two subsidiary companies, Alert Management Systems Inc. and Pan American World Airways. Along with U.S. relatives of disaster victims, the Smiths are being represented by a firm of lawyers who specialize in aviation litigation—Speiser, Krause & Madole, who have offices near the White House in Washington and, coincidentally, in the Pan Am Building in Manhattan. When these cases eventually come to court in the early 1990s—some in federal courts, the Smiths' in the Florida State Court—the lead trial lawyer will be that firm's senior partner, Don Madole, a U.S. Navy reserve commander with years of experience flying warplanes from aircraft carriers and a track record of aviation cases that fills most of a large sheet of paper.

Madole says that the Warsaw Convention is completely out of date and needs to be done away with. "We don't have any fledgling airlines carrying people across the Atlantic, do we? It's a big business game."

It is the contention of the relatives of those who died that airlines use the Warsaw Convention as a foil against having to pay sufficient attention to security to avoid disasters such as Lockerbie. They point to the number of attempted bombings that have been prevented by El Al security, and ask why their methods are not more generally employed.

One of the problems in international aviation is that the large corporations are now run by second- and third-generation management—products of Harvard Business School and similar establishments—whose aim is to show at least a little profit each quarter. It is said that this slavedom to the accounts is what has made security the aviation backwater that it appears to have become.

Under American law, an airline is required to exercise the highest standard of care. It was in the climate following the U.S. bombing raid on Libya that Pan Am made the application for the security surcharge. As we have seen, Pan Am advertised their improved security measures as a method of attracting passengers when U.S. citizens were reluctant to fly overseas for fear of retaliation for the Tripoli raids. When the cases come to court, lawyers will say that the warnings issued by the FAA should have ensured an even higher standard of care over safety.

Pan Am has, to date, settled one compensation claim arising from the Lockerbie crash. They've paid $59,000 to Captain Bruce Smith, a Pan Am pilot, for the loss of his

wife, Ingrid. Other settlements of $100,000 have been of-
fered, but so far no relative has accepted.

Don Madole says that he will be pressing for damages
far in excess of these figures. "Assuming there was negligence, just assuming, what you have is the family unity
that is broken up, the son who will never receive the arm
around the shoulder after he does something well at
school. Is society supposed to handle this, or should people who had the duty, should those people be required to
pay for the loss of the support to the family?"

The test for lawyers under the Warsaw Convention is
one of "willful misconduct"—in broad terms, the airlines
recognizing the risk and not doing enough about it. Lawyers in Britain and the United States realize that the fight
will be a tough one, but they say that if they can prove
willful misconduct, it will have a profound effect on airline
security generally. They are convinced that if their cases
are proved, governments will have to take steps to improve
air security. They say that aircraft are such obvious targets
that more should be done to protect them.

The compensation levels of the Warsaw Convention
are amended by international protocols agreed between
the signatory states at regular (if long) intervals. The last
time the Convention was altered was at a meeting in Mon-
treal in 1975. Then the upper level for death in an aircraft
accident was increased from $75,000 to roughly $500,000.
However, in the decade and a half since it was agreed, the
amendment has not yet been ratified by the necessary
thirty nations to bring it into effect. So the official maximum that an airline must pay remains at $75,000, a totally
unrealistic level of compensation for the loss of life of a

breadwinner. It seems that Pan Am, by offering Captain Smith $59,000 and higher amounts to other relatives, has at least taken in the spirit of the Montreal protocol, though these offers are nowhere near the compensation levels that could be given in an American court if negligence against the airline is proved.

As Paul Hudson, the New York lawyer who lost his daughter Melina on Flight 103, and the other relatives fought to have the circumstances of the Lockerbie crash investigated by a full public inquiry, their anger and concern focused on the Helsinki warning, the only warning they knew to be in force up to December 21. Then, on what many of the relatives call "the blackest day of them all," 16 March 1989, it was revealed that the FAA and other aviation bodies had indeed circulated warnings following the PFLP-GC raids and had given details of the barometric device found then.

Two days before this was revealed, Samuel K. Skinner, the U.S. Transportation Secretary, and Ambassador Clayton E. McManaway of the State Department, had both testified to a Senate subcommittee. They went through what relatives now regard as a near charade, not mentioning the PFLP-GC warnings and allowing the subcommittee to concentrate solely on the Helsinki warning. It was during this hearing that McManaway made the now hotly disputed assertion that the Helsinki warning had been regarded as a hoax by December 10.

He and Skinner both went to great lengths to say that the partial publication of the Helsinki warning had been a regrettable breach of regulations that should not have happened. There had been no intention of warning only government employees and not the general public about the possibility of a terrorist attack on a Pan Am flight.

McManaway went further. He said that if there had been a concerted effort to warn government employees about the danger flights, then the State Department employees returning from Lebanon would not have been on Flight 103. The allegation that government staff had been tipped off was, according to McManaway, "something that has plagued us. That bulletin should not have been given out."

A senator then stated to McManaway: "Anyone who did not see it [the bulletin] would have been at a disadvantage."

"Yes, but all Pan Am flights were 'targets.'"

Skinner told the hearing that he did not think there had been a deliberate attempt by Pan Am to fill up the flight by offering discounted tickets for seats that, the relatives allege, had been left vacant by State Department employees canceling reservations and flying with other American carriers.

New York Republican Senator Alfonse D'Amato said that he saw a double standard, telling government staff of the warning but not the public. He asked if, in retrospect, Skinner believed that the public should have been warned of the Helsinki threat. Skinner said no. Should the crew have been informed? "They are—of significant threats," Skinner replied. Were the crew of Flight 103 informed? "No."

Skinner did say that if there was a credible threat against a U.S. airline and, despite being warned, the airline did not increase security sufficiently to counter the threat, or if the threat was not able to be countered, the Department of Transportation would ask the airline to cancel the flight or flights. If they did not, said Skinner, then the public would be informed. He said that this had never happened before.

The handling by the State Department of the U.S. relatives of the dead also came under attack at that March 14 hearing. Relatives had complained that they had been unable to get any help at all from the Department. In its defense, McManaway cited the fact that State Department officials at Lockerbie ran up eight hundred hours in overtime coping with the aftermath. Senate subcommittee chairman Frank Lautenberg replied that he thought it outrageous that, here, they were dealing with the worst act of terrorism against citizens of the United States, and their representatives overseas were counting up the overtime.

Also giving evidence at that hearing was Bert Ammerman. He told the subcommittee that as far as he was able to determine, all the State Department officials had done was to stamp death certificates to allow bodies to be repatriated to the United States. After a spirited half-hour defense of the State Department, Ambassador McManaway stood up and unreservedly apologized to the relatives and promised a full inquiry.

After those hearings the relatives felt that they had achieved a partial victory in just one of the many battles they would face in their fight to improve air security. That mood was destroyed completely by the revelations that were to follow just forty-eight hours later.

On 16 March 1989 news of the main warning about

the PFLP-GC raid broke, and it became clear that the airlines had had information in their possession that could have prevented Flight 103 being blown out of the sky.

At the time, Bert Ammerman said: "The U.S. government and the British government have been hanging their hats on this December fifth warning to Helsinki, saying that was a hoax. Now it is clear there were six or seven warnings that could have been tied in together. Because, on Thursday, the U.S. government and the British government made these announcements about something they had not mentioned until this point, we are now demanding an independent investigation of Pan Am Flight 103. It is obvious that they are getting all the information, all the skeletons out of the closet now because they know there are going to be hearings and they are going to be held accountable."

Ammerman says starkly: "There is no such thing as airport security. All we are doing is to try and counter the situation and save more people going through what we are going through."

Recent newspaper-inspired breaches of U.K. airport security would tend to support Ammerman's contention. Even after Flight 103, journalists from various publications and television programs have been able to run rings around security procedures by gaining jobs that allow access to aircraft and sensitive areas of airports with only minimal checks being made on them.

U.S. Transportation Secretary Skinner says that the lesson to be learned from Flight 103—and from the other terrorist bombings of aircraft, Air India Flight 182, TWA Flight 840, and Korean Air Flight 858—is that "we must continue to build on the solid foundation of security measures built over the last decade and a half. We must continue to evolve strong, yet flexible approaches that will bring our best technology and best people to bear on this problem. The process of reviewing, refining, and redirecting aviation security must be continuous."

According to Skinner, the world's terrorist movements have moved away from hijacking into bombing in the past several years. The undisputed fact is that, in world terms, terrorists are beating governments 4–1. There has been only one bomb attempt averted recently: Nezar Hindawi's 1986 attack on the El Al flight from London to Tel Aviv. This attack was thwarted by El Al security.

Isaac Yeffet, the man responsible for devising El Al's security, says: "You cannot X-ray a full load of luggage. You won't see anything apart from some dark pictures or the work of some amateur who's put a crude device inside the luggage. The terrorist is sophisticated and he knows how to conceal explosives inside luggage. So if you want to X-ray and come up with results, you must open up luggage. Then you might see the bomb."

It is Yeffet's belief that the Flight 103 disaster happened solely because of lax security. If there had been an adequate level of security, the tragedy might have been prevented. Security hangs on motivation, dedication, and regular exercises to keep the system on its toes.

Recently some U.S. airports introduced security bonuses to keep operatives alert. Suspect items are deliberately sent through the system, and if they are picked out, the security officer responsible can win a bonus of $1,000.

Yeffet says that security personnel have to be convinced that they are responsible for the safety of every 747 and its four hundred passengers. They are the front line against the terrorist.

Even after Lockerbie this would not appear to be happening. The *Sun* newspaper reporter George Pascoe Watson managed to get a job as a Pan Am baggage handler at Heathrow. He was able to secure employment with only minimal checks being made on him before he was cleared for entry to sensitive areas of the airport.

For security experts the more alarming part of Pascoe Watson's story was the way in which he observed security for Pan Am being handled. He said that the X-ray machine operatives behind the scenes at Heathrow appeared to be of a very low caliber. In the two days that he worked there, he saw little evidence of concerted attempts being made to check what was in bags—only on one occasion was a suspect bag opened. In addition, the X-ray operative worked eight-hour shifts with only minimal breaks away from the screen.

Former British Airways security boss Dennis Phipps says that the recommended time on a machine is only twenty minutes in any one stretch, and then at least forty minutes must be spent on other duties away from the screen.

Yeffet is convinced that, even post-Lockerbie, airlines are wide open for a repeat performance of the bombing of Flight 103. He says that although he is now out of the official side of the business, casual observation at a major airport would give him sufficient knowledge to have a well-constructed explosive device loaded onto a plane with no difficulty. "I do not believe they can have built security so fast. It is not at such a level that luggage with an explosive device will not just be sent to the aircraft as with 103. Until they have well-trained, well-motivated people, I won't be surprised if some other aircraft blows up."

That possibility is so real in Yeffet's mind that he has broken a media silence stretching back throughout his career. He says that for nearly thirty years he has refused all offers of media interviews. Now he is willing not only to be interviewed, but also to cooperate with media attempts to show how lax security is at airports. In the March issue of *Life* magazine Yeffet toured U.S. airports and wrote a damning account of how unsecure the system is. For the price of a small bribe to luggage handlers, he had suitcases flown to the destination of his choice—without him accompanying it. To have luggage sent without the trouble of a bribe, he picked up baggage labels left carelessly lying around.

He says that no attempts are made in the U.S. to reconcile the number of passengers on a plane with the number who have checked in, which means that suitcases can fly without their owners, leaving the way open for a terrorist. He warns that if European airports tighten their security to a high and effective level, terrorists wanting to hit the United States will move into that country and find nothing to bar their way.

Until last year responsibility for security at Pan Am lay with Harry Pizer, one of the corporation's vice-presidents, who retired at the age of seventy-two. Yeffet describes him as a "nice man" but says that no security man can do his job properly unless he is in a position to tell his chairman, "To do the job, we need X, Y, and Z." Whether or not Pizer had that level of influence, Yeffet doesn't know.

"Another example," continues Yeffet, "is that you cannot assign the station manager of one airline also to be responsible for security. Immediately, he has a conflict between the two jobs. On one hand, he wants to keep the aircraft departing on time; on the other, [he is] in charge of security [and] must realize the need for delay if it is needed. This kind of conflict is very bad for security."

This conflict was graphically illustrated in Pan Am's own house magazine, *The Pan Am Clipper*. A recent issue had a page 1 story and a center-spread follow-up on how the company coped with the aftermath of Lockerbie. At the bottom of page 1 was an article describing the drive for prompt departure of key flights. Senior vice-president Tony Mule is quoted as saying:

> It has been proven time and time again that a passenger's first real measure of airline performance is whether his or her flight departs when the schedule says it is going to depart . . . All they know is they plan to be on time and expect Pan Am to keep them on time. When departure time comes and goes and the plane is still on the gate, their on-time consideration may well become a serious concern.
>
> That concern can result in a letter or a call to the Department of Transportation, and that becomes a black mark on Pan Am's record for the public to see.

The lengthy article continues by outlining the systems that have been devised to improve time performance. In thirty-two column inches, the word "security" does not appear until the end of the article; in the final paragraphs, Mule concedes that the complete screening of baggage means extra time added to travelers' journey times.

A delay in boarding, a delay in loading bags or cargo, a delay in fueling or obtaining the flight plan, can mean far more than a simple delay in one 747 destined for JFK. A single delay on a kickoff flight can inconvenience hundreds of passengers at a principal hub [network airport] and can cost Pan Am thousands of dollars.

On April 17 I called Pan Am reservations in London and asked what was the last check-in time for that night's six P.M. Flight 003 to JFK (Flight 003 is the newly renumbered Flight 103).

"Two hours before departure," I was told.

"Is that inflexible? I think it'll be a little later than that before I can get to Heathrow."

"Well, an hour and a half before should be sufficient."

"But I don't think I can get there until about five, maybe just after."

"Well, don't make it any later than that," came back the advice.

If X rays are not the solution to beating the bombers, then what is? The airline industry is pinning its hopes on thermal-neutron-analysis machines. These TNA machines, pioneered in the United States, are capable of detecting all commercial and military explosives that might be concealed in checked-in baggage and air cargo. Tests carried out for the FAA show the success rate of the devices to be around 95 percent, with a 4 percent false-alarm rate. The FAA tests were carried out on thirty thousand items of baggage, and the amount of explosives used in any of them was very small. Scientists say that if the weights of explosives had been the same as those capable of causing aircraft failure, their detection rate would have been much higher.

Work is also being done on a vapor detection system for checking people with explosives. Again tests are promising, but the time that it takes to check each passenger—about thirty seconds—is deemed too long, and further work is being done to reduce this to around six seconds.

The FAA reckons that an effective system of TNA machines at key airports worldwide to help protect American airlines could be in place within two years, at a cost of around $159 million.

The International Foundation of Airline Passengers Associations, a Swiss-based lobby for travelers, is calling for the establishment of a billion-dollar fund to improve air security. Its plan is to surcharge every airline passenger by one dollar and use the money raised to improve and then police air security worldwide, with a particular emphasis on the airports of developing countries. It is their contention that every airport has to be safe, otherwise weak points in the chain would be identified and used to perpetrate acts of terrorism. The fund would also help finance research into new techniques for beating the bombers.

13

MASS MURDER
UNPUNISHED

"Sooner or later there has to be a conclusion."

For the detectives in Scotland satisfaction will come only when the person or persons responsible for the Lockerbie bombing appear in the dock of the High Court in Edinburgh. This will most likely not happen.

Apart from any other consideration, if the culprit(s) is arrested in a country that is likely to extradite him, the Americans would try to have him brought to their country for trial. They have, in the past, gone to great lengths to capture terrorists who have committed crimes against U.S. citizens, even spiriting one man out of Beirut to stand trial in Washington for the hijacking of a Jordanian passenger jet that carried only three Americans, none of whom was injured in the incident.

The most likely conclusion to the investigation is for Scottish law enforcement officials to announce the identity of the bomber(s) and the group or groups behind them. Some act of retaliation would almost certainly follow.

The ultimate responsibility for the investigation of the Lockerbie disaster lies with Scotland's senior law officer, the Lord Advocate, Peter Fraser of Carmylie. He has instructed the police to pursue their inquiries, as in any other criminal investigation, to build up a forensic case, but he readily agrees that the huge amount of intelligence gathered by covert agencies is giving definite lines to pursue. As Lord Advocate he is, under Scottish law, in charge of all prosecutions. The police report on major cases to his office and, in return, the Lord Advocate and his deputies direct investigations.

The breakthrough will come when police finally identify the individual who carried the bomb onto the plane. Senior officers on the case are convinced that that person was entirely innocent of any complicity in the outrage and would have been duped one way or another. It may be that the carrier thought there were drugs in whatever was given to him or her, but senior officers think this unlikely. They believe that Jabril's men stuck to their tried-and-tested method of getting bombs on planes: one of the members of the West German PFLP-GC cell would have befriended a woman and asked her to take the Toshiba cassette recorder to America as a Christmas present for relatives.

The process of finding out which passenger had the bomb has been extremely difficult. The police have revealed publicly that they know the type of luggage in which the bomb was held, but because that material is commonly used in the manufacture of a common, inexpensive brand of luggage—Samsonite—they have been so far unable to narrow down the owner of that particular suitcase to an individual passenger. One of the reasons so much luggage and personal property has been held at Lockerbie's Dexstar warehouse is because until that passenger is identified, detectives have no idea what clues they may lose forever by returning that property to relatives. Indeed, after the case was found to be a Samsonite, a new search of the baggage in the warehouse revealed further fragments of the "bomb bag" mixed up with other belongings.

Detailed and painstaking inquiries into the backgrounds of every passenger who boarded the flight at Frankfurt have narrowed the list of "suspects" who might have carried the bomb to three women who are known to have been friendly with Palestinians in West Germany. When detectives are certain which one of the three carried the bomb, they will make this information public, mainly as a humanitarian act to the relatives of the other 258 people who died in the disaster. They must all have a nagging worry that it was perhaps their loved one who made the fatal mistake by doing what they supposed was a simple act of kindness that was repaid in mass slaughter.

Most of the speculation as to the identity of the bomb carrier has centered on Lebanese student Khaled Jafaar. However, Jafaar was perhaps the least likely passenger to be given a bomb to carry. Although a U.S. citizen, he was of Lebanese origin. He had flown into Frankfurt from Baalbeck, a notorious hideout for terrorists. Even the barest minimum of security and profiling of passengers would have discovered that he was the prime candidate for detailed searching. In addition, his father is certain that Khaled Jafaar had no checked luggage, just two soft bags carried onto the plane.

Peter Fraser says that it has been the painstaking examination of the bodies and the luggage that has allowed the investigation to reach the advanced stage it is at now. He is only too well aware that attention to detail was also the source of grief for many of the relatives, who suffered long delays in having the bodies of their loved ones released for burial.

The visit to America by Deputy Chief Constable Paul Newell and other officers alleviated that anger, leaving relatives with a clear understanding of how important were the reasons for those delays. Lord Fraser says: "They [the relatives] alternate in their emotions and their desires at a time of terrible crisis for them. They want the bodies of their relatives home so they can have a proper funeral, they want their belongings back, and a number of them who I have seen and have written to me are in conflict. They want their rings and so on, and we have to say, 'I'm sorry, we have to check these things out,' and they say, 'Absolutely, we understand that, it is quite right. If there is a detail that will help track down these people, we understand that.' "

The world's intelligence elite are hardly likely to share the innermost secrets of their anti-terrorist operations with a Glasgow policeman. Intelligence agencies are notorious for their involvement in political games in the same way as their political masters, and they will be selective with their dissemination of information to help more mainstream political operations.

Peter Fraser is aware of this, but says that he has no reason to think that anything vital to the Lockerbie inquiry has been held back. "There really has been a very useful flow of intelligence. I have no doubt, though, that there are bits of it that have been held back, and I would expect them to be held back, in the same way that, in a domestic context, a policeman may say that an informer has told him to look in a certain direction. That's not evidence, but it is a useful pointer, and we would not then turn 'round to that policeman and say, 'Who is your informer? How does he know?' "

To the Lord Advocate's legal mind, only hard and concrete evidence sustainable in a court of law is sufficient to identify the bomber(s), and is certainly needed before any public statement on how the bombing was carried out can be made. He says that he still has no concrete evidence to show that the bomb was placed on the plane at Frankfurt. There is still a possibility that a corrupted baggage handler at Heathrow Airport slipped the case into the Frankfurt baggage. But because of the weight of evidence already unearthed, he says that the police would be "bloody silly" if they did not make the most detailed inquiries at the Frankfurt end.

What are the chances of a culprit being identified and standing between two policemen in a courtroom dock? The Lord Advocate says: "Put it this way. If the bomb had gone off ten minutes later and the plane had fallen into the sea and we recovered nothing, that would be very remote indeed. The fact that we have recovered from 840 square miles of southern Scotland the thousands of items that have been examined, I would have to say that I am quite surprised that we have got as far as we have done with this quite incredible forensic work that has been undertaken.

"That being so, I have no reason to exclude the possibility that we will identify even more precisely the suitcase, its ownership, and its point of introduction." There he stops.

The Lord Advocate asserts firmly that, even though there may well be good reasons for not finding out exactly who bombed Flight 103—primarily the likely effects on Middle East peace moves—he is under no pressure whatsoever to "take a dive on this one."

"Although I am a member of this government, I am a law officer and my role is clearly understood. Any attempt to put political pressure on me would meet with a very dusty response, but there has been none.

"I would be naive and inexperienced if I was not very conscious of the political ramifications of this. The very fact of a successful outcome to the investigation, if it is achieved, might have political tensions. [If it had happened,] say, in Amsterdam, and it transpires that all the security men were at a Christmas party, it is not difficult to see political tensions between Holland and the U.S. and U.K. if they had failed to observe proper procedures." That, he stresses, is only meant as an example with no fact behind it.

And the Lord Advocate is only too well aware of the wider, and more real, problem of identifying any state, or states, behind the bombing. "Clearly there are those sort of questions. If it is Syrian-inspired, Egyptian-inspired, or Libyan-inspired, it is not difficult to see that fitting this into international relations is going to be extremely tricky."

But, he says, if you read the American press, the pressure that President Bush and the CIA are under to come up with a solution to the investigation is very apparent. "If there were those who thought it would be better to find out who did it but not say too much about it, they would have to weigh up that there is a far greater political force and pressure in the American domestic scene."

There will be no naming of the group behind the attack from official sources until the Lord Advocate has a case that is as near as possible to one sustainable in law. "Sooner or later, there has to be a conclusion to this. If the criminal investigation comes to nought, there will have to be an inquiry of some sort. I'm not avoiding that at the moment, but I'm anxious not to excite it because I have no intention of arranging to do anything until my criminal investigation has reached a successful conclusion or a point where, reluctantly, we can't go any further because the trail has gone cold. There will have to be a point where we have to say pretty fully what we know. That does not include what may be high-quality intelligence speculation, but what we have established as fact.

"We are not at that stage. I am not anxious to excite any jurisdictional battle. The international cooperation we are receiving is pretty good, and I don't want to say to any country that may be interested, 'In no circumstances will I hand over to you the evidence we have accumulated.'

"I am not interested in that scene at the moment. If we get to the scene of saying 'Those are the people we want,' I think those of us who have the respect of prosecutorial responsibilities will say, 'Now let's look at this and see how best to do it.'"

Those words support the theory of some observers who say that because of America's greater political muscle in the world, it may be that the U.S. is in a better position to lever a none-too-friendly country into extraditing suspects. There is, however, one powerful argument against this: some countries that have abolished the death penalty will not extradite suspects to the U.S. because of the likelihood of a convicted bomber being executed.

However, for now, the police inquiry goes on, having already run up bills in the region of £5 million [approximately $8.5 million]. It is likely to continue for many months, until, as Peter Fraser puts it, the trail goes cold.

For the people of Lockerbie that means many more months of the still large police presence in the town. For Lockerbie Academy pupils it means many more months of science experiments in makeshift cabins in the school parking lot, the inside labs having been taken over by the police team. That is a source of great annoyance to school rector Andrew Blake. There had originally been talk of bussing the Lockerbie pupils to Dumfries to allow police to retain use of the whole Academy building, but Mr. Blake says that suggestion was dropped for fear of a major outcry.

In the days before the school reopened after the Christmas vacation, a compromise was reached allowing police to retain an annex. "In the space of five days," says the rector, "they put up these Portacabins at a cost equivalent to building a small primary school. It annoyed the local people, it was bound to. They ripped out two very good laboratories, which, to most people from outside, seemed to be a nonsense. I mean, why couldn't the police go into the Portacabins? But with their political push, they got what they wanted."

The presence of the police means that, as the physical scars left by the crash are healed, the mental ones are kept in the forefront of people's minds, since they see detectives strolling the streets of the town during lunch breaks and police vehicles going to and fro.

At the moment there are good grounds to keep the investigation based in the town. New inquiries come up each day that require further checking in the locality. A great deal of property is still being stored, sifted, and rechecked at Dexstar. The day will come, though, when these inquiries are exhausted, the property is at last returned, and then, probably, detectives will pack up their paperwork and head north to reestablish the inquiry at Glasgow.

The police presence apart, life in Lockerbie is returning to as near normal as possible. In the pubs, the events of 21 December 1988 are no longer the sole topic of conversation. They are rarely mentioned, in fact, until a stranger comes into the bar and inevitably starts asking questions. Talk of the disaster now mainly centers on the distribution of the £1.8 million [approximately $3 million] disaster fund, the result of an outpouring of public donations for the Lockerbie residents affected by the catastrophe. The trustees decided to allocate payments of up to £1000 [$1,700] for the "shock and trauma" experienced by people who lived in and around the worst-affected areas of the town. That has led to disputes along the lines of "Why has so and so been paid £1000 and my mother just two doors away got nothing?"

But the disaster fund is doing much good work. Many people in Sherwood Crescent were underinsured, and while disputes with Pan Am and their insurers continue, the fund is paying out to make sure that proper repairs are done to homes as quickly as possible. In March the crater, where once three houses stood, was filled in and trees planted above. There will have to be a memorial in the town for the many Americans who feel drawn to Lockerbie, their loved ones' last place on earth. Many in the town do not want one, fearing it will attract sightseers to what are essentially private residential areas. A memorial will, however, be built.

The site of Ella Ramsden's former home is one favored location. Mrs. Ramsden does not go back to Park Place these days. She has been rehoused across town in Kintail Park, and says she's become a "Kintaily" now that her old home and her possessions are gone. She does not grieve for them. She is totally practical and is content to build anew, her sentimentality of ownership replaced by a warmth generated by the kindness shown to her by total strangers in the days after the crash that so nearly claimed her life.

One appearance on a television news bulletin prompted hundreds of letters and donations from all over the country. All this gave her the strength and, to a less extent, the money to help her carry on. It does not take much prompting for Mrs. Ramsden to go into the cupboard of her new living room and bring out bags full of letters, each one carefully answered, to demonstrate the kindness that she has been shown.

That kindness has been demonstrated over and over again in acts of generosity toward the people of Lockerbie from all quarters: free trips to the pantomime for the children, holidays for old folks, benefit concerts for the disaster fund.

The desire for as much normality as circumstances allow has spread over the entire town. The whist drives go on. Bingo night is still Wednesday. Rector Andrew Blake says that the wish to have things as they were before is a result of a conscious decision. "We were very determined that we would run the school, as far as possible, as normal. But we started to get that feeling, *it's not normal.*

"I was under quite a lot of pressure to have in-depth counseling of staff and pupils, and rightly or wrongly— and rightly, I think, as it has turned out—I took the view that young people are young people and you don't alter that. They all have characteristics in common, and one of the characteristics is that young people do not sit back and talk about the past. They are thinking about the future. What happens in the past affects what they think about the future, but no more than that."

The decision was taken to operate the school as normally as possible, but staff were to be alert to any potential problems. There was a natural apprehension, for example, over the return to school of Stephen Flannigan. Also in his class had been Paul Somerville, who lost his life in the crash. "As it is with young people, you do not need to be apprehensive. If you are, for instance, not sure what to say to someone, that is quite normal. If an acquaintance loses someone it is quite normal, if you're walking along the street, to cross over because you're not sure what to say. As long as it's accepted as a normal reaction, people are not surprised by it. They may be embarrassed, but not surprised."

Mr. Blake says that as far as he is aware, you wouldn't realize by walking around the school that Lockerbie had suffered a disaster. Pupils have neither been encouraged nor discouraged to talk or write about or draw pictures of the disaster. Nothing has transpired, he says, that can directly be attributed to the disaster. "I'm under no illusions, though. The likes of Stephen Flannigan are still okay, but he has a lot of water to put under the bridge yet. Whether it hits him gradually or whether it hits him suddenly, we don't know yet, but for the majority of people, it has almost passed."

In the days following the disaster, one young mother worried that the crash might have had a profound effect on her children. They had stopped playing cowboys and Indians and other traditional games in favor of playing at being helicopter pilots. She considered whether there were possible sinister psychological factors behind the change, but eventually she concluded that this sort of play was really quite normal, as her kids had been seeing nothing but helicopters for days and days. She felt that it would no doubt pass, and it has. "It had nothing to do with an emotional reaction," she reports.

Doctors in the town, though, say that the weak point in many people, old and young alike, is loud noise. People still have unusually severe reactions to the normal bangs that occur in any town.

As the days passed after the Lockerbie explosion, and airport security was breached by journalists and assailed by critics, determined efforts were made by the U.K. Transport Department to tighten things up. The advice given out by the department has varied from practical guides to assertions that have, to say the least, surprised airline bosses. One of the latter was the direction from the department's principal security advisor that suspicious items should not be allowed into the passenger cabins of planes, but consigned to the hold.

As the story of the warnings unfolded, Transport Secretary Paul Channon looked increasingly vulnerable and his resignation was confidently expected. However, it was not to come. The drive for improved security culminated at the end of April in a declaration from the minister that he is to seek new powers from Parliament to improve air security generally.

The research budget for new X-ray and explosive-sniffing devices was doubled to £1 million [approximately $1.7 million], and urgent consideration was given to an offer from the FAA for the loan of a TNA explosive-sniffing machine to Heathrow Airport. In the event, the Department of Transport has decided to install the loaned device at Gatwick. The department says, however, that because the machines rely on thermal-neutron activation, considerable problems of radiation-protection arise. New rules are also being introduced to require the screening and X-raying of all cargo and hold baggage on flights deemed to be at a higher risk than normal.

However, the department says that it has no intention of introducing El Al–style security. "Security measures must be in line with the threat," says a spokesman. "The extreme measures used by El Al are appropriate for dealing with an extreme threat, but would not be justified for most operations."

While there is, of course, international action that can

be carried out to try and beat the bombers, Paul Channon can suggest legislation only for Britain. And as security is enhanced, it has to be done so against a background of overcrowded airports already putting through far too many passengers every day, in buildings that have not been designed in the main to cope with a high level of security.

Isaac Yeffet is extremely doubtful of the ability of machinery to counter the threat of airline bombings. Machines cannot, he says, ask questions. It is proper training in that direction that holds the key to safe air travel, allied to technology. "Machines cannot tell me that there is something suspicious in the passenger's face. If you smuggle jewelery, money, or drugs, it will show in the face. The terrorist, or smuggler, does not know what questions are to be asked. If I'm asking the right questions in a professional way, and you lie because you are hiding something in the luggage, psychological changes will take place in the face and give the smuggler up."

While that sort of interrogation does not, of course, work for the dupe, questioning of innocent couriers could quickly establish whether they were carrying an item with which they were not entirely conversant. "It may just be a paling of the complexion," says Yeffet, "a drying of the lips, a lack of cooperation."

No matter what steps are taken to try and stop future bomb attacks, sophisticated terrorists will try to beat them and attack the easiest and most exposed target of any country: a civilian aircraft. The balance has to be weighed between total security and speedy air travel. The harsh reality of Lockerbie is that, in world terms, it will in a short time be consigned to textbooks as another example of the workings of terrorists. If it were not for the campaigning of the relatives in the United States and Britain, that process would be well under way. They are asking the tough questions that governments and the airline industry either do not want to answer or feel they must not answer in the name of security. It is clear that the Lockerbie disaster was foreseeable—it was foreseen. It was avoidable, but it was not avoided.

Much has been made and is being made by transportation departments in Britain and the United States of the new rules and procedures being considered and introduced. It comes as no comfort to the grieving relatives to realize, as they increasingly do, that on December 21 the rule books of international air travel contained sufficient protection, if properly enforced, to beat the bombers.

It is the low emphasis that was placed on security internationally in the time prior to the disaster that allowed the slaughter of the innocents. It is the simple facts that cost 270 lives. It is the fact that security is a low-paid job attracting low-caliber personnel insufficiently trained to carry out their jobs properly. As Yeffet has said, each and every security operative is responsible for the lives of a planeload of human beings each time he or she sits down at the X-ray machine. With this lack of professionalism, even complete screening of all checked aircraft baggage will be no guarantee that there will not be another Lockerbie.

The consuming fear of all who have been involved one way or another in the events surrounding the Lockerbie disaster is that there may well be another. There is little to stand in the way of the determined terrorist, certainly not the security overhauls that have taken place and are still under way.

Many feel that the risk of being bombed out of the sky in a terrorist attack is so remote that they are happy to have the convenience of turning up just before takeoff. This was demonstrated by an incident that occured shortly after the bombing of Flight 103. Pan Am received a bomb warning for one of their flights from New York. The aircraft was searched and, uniquely, the passengers were informed of the threat and given the chance of taking another flight. Only eighteen people opted out.

The remoteness of being involved in a plane bombing is such that, less than three months after Lockerbie, when I flew in a jumbo jet right over the disaster town en route to New York, it barely affected me. Unlike Flight 103, this day it was still light, and there was not a cloud in the sky as the Air France plane cruised over the Scottish border at a height of around 31,000 feet, just as the *Maid of the Seas* had done in December. Despite weeks of working almost exclusively on the Lockerbie story, I felt near total detachment as, first, a sunbathed Tundergarth church, and then the town itself, passed underneath. It was, and still is, totally impossible to begin to imagine what happened on that plane that night.

What is not impossible to imagine, and is the stuff of nightmares, is that there will be another Lockerbie. The plane may not fall on a town, but once more terrorism will claim the lives of innocent air travelers.

The Lockerbie bombing was an outrage of world proportions. Its motive may never become clear. Vengeance for the *Vincennes* shooting down of the airbus? Palestinian disdain for the events in the Middle East? Both will have a part somewhere in the tragedy. In real terms, though, little has changed. The Middle East peace progress stumbles along. Arafat and the PLO continue their rehabilitation.

However, the one thing that has clearly been affected is air travel. In the words of Mao Zedong, "Kill one, scare a thousand," and Pan Am bookings have certainly been hit. It may well be that airlines will come to the conclusion that safety and security *are* selling points. Pan Am tried it in 1986, but whether or not it worked is hard to define. El Al, with its three-hour security check before every flight, has certainly found it lucrative; there is maximum occupancy for each of the flights on its limited number of routes. It may be that bigger carriers with more planes to more destinations may see this as an effective marketing strategy.

The only certain conclusion from the entire Lockerbie disaster is that not one of those 270 people deserved to die. The people settling down for their journey to New York and Detroit did not deserve to die. The people in Lockerbie going about their everyday lives in festively bedecked homes did not deserve to be wiped from the face of the earth just four days before Christmas.

The fact that it is now almost a cliché does not detract from the veracity of the statement that for Lockerbie, Christmas can never be the same again. Christmas 1989 will bring with it the media army that descended on the town a year before—this time for the "first anniversary" pieces. One of the poignant facts that will no doubt be highlighted is that, twelve months after the disaster, still no perpetrator has been identified publicly.

For friends and relatives of the passengers of Flight 103, Christmas, that most joyous time of the year, will bring with it memories of that sad and pointless loss of their loved ones. There will be tears and anger, there may even be forgiveness and compassion, but there will never be, and can never be, understanding.

THE VICTIMS OF PAN AM
FLIGHT 103

AIRLINE STAFF

Cockpit crew

Captain: MacQuarrie, James Bruce, 55, Kensington, New Hampshire, USA. American
First Officer: Wagner, Raymond Ronald, 52, Pennington, New Jersey, USA. American
Flight Engineer: Avritt, Jerry Don, 46, Westminster, California, USA. American

Pursers

Murphy, Mary Geraldine, 51, Twickenham, England. British
Velimirovich, Milutin, 35, Hounslow, England. Czechoslovakian

Flight attendants

ENGSTROM, Siv Ulla, 51, Windsor, England. Swedish
AVOYNE, Elisabeth Nichole, 44, Croissy sur Seine, France.
French
BERTI, Noelle Lydie, 41, Paris, France. French
KUHNE, Elke Etha, 43, Hanover, West Germany. West
German
LARRACOECHEA, Maria Nieves, 39, Madrid, Spain. Spanish
ish
GARRETT, Paul Isaac, 41, Napa, California, USA. American
can
ROYAL, Myra Josephine, 30, Hanwell, London, England.
Dominican Republic
FRANKLIN, Stacie Denise, 20, San Diego, USA. American
SKABO, Irja Syhnove, 38, Oslo, Norway. Finnish
McALOLOOY, Lilibeth Tobila, 27, Kelsterback, West Germany. Filipino
many. Filipino
REINA, Jocelyn, 26, Isleworth, Middlesex, England. American
can

PASSENGERS

AHERN, John Michael Gerard, 26, New York City, USA.
American
AICHER, Sarah Margaret, 29, London, England. American
AKERSTROM, John David, 34, Medina, Ohio, USA. American
can
ALEXANDER, Ronald Ely, 46, New York City, USA. Swiss
AMMERMAN, Thomas Joseph, 36, Old Tappan, New
Jersey, USA. American

APFELBAUM, Martin Lewis, 59, Philadelphia, USA. American

ASRELSKY, Rachel Marie, 21, New York City, USA. American

ATKINSON, Judith Ellen, 37, London, England. American
ATKINSON, William Garreston, 33, London, England. American

BACCIOCHI, Clare Louise, 19, Tamworth, England. British
BAINBRIDGE, Harry Michael, 34, Montrose, New York, USA. American

BARCLAY, Stuart Murray, 29, Farm Barnard, Vermont, USA. Canadian

BELL, Jean Mary, 44, Windsor, England. British
BENELLO, Julian MacBain, 26, Brookline, Massachusetts, USA. American

BENNETT, Lawrence Ray, 41, Chelsea, Michigan, USA. American

BERGSTROM, Philip Vernon, 22, Forest Lake, Minnesota, USA. American

BERKLEY, Alistair David, 29, London, England. British
BERNSTEIN, Michael Stuart, 36, Bethesda, Maryland, USA. American

BERRELL, Steven Russell, 20, Fargo, North Dakota, USA. American

BHATIA, Surinder Mohan, 51, Los Angeles, California, USA. Indian

BISSETT, Kenneth John, 21, Hartsdale, New York, USA. American

BOATMAN-FULLER, Diane Ann, 35, London, England. American

BOLAND, Stephen John, 20, Nashua, New Hampshire, USA. American

BOUCKLEY, Glen John, 27, Liverpool, New York, USA. British

BOUCKLEY, Paula Marie, 29, Liverpool, New York, USA. American

BOULANGER, Nicole Elise, 21, Shrewsbury, Massachusetts, USA. American

BOYER, Francis, 43, Toulosane, France. French

BRIGHT, Nicholas, 32, Brookline, Massachusetts, USA. American

BROWNER (BIER), Daniel Solomon, 23, Parod, Israel. Israeli

BRUNNER, Colleen Renee, 20, Hamburg, New York, USA. American

BURMAN, Timothy Guy, 24, London, England. British

BUSER, Michael Warren, 34, Richfield Park, New Jersey, USA. American

BUSER, Warren Max, 62, Glenrock, New Jersey, USA. American

BUTLER, Steven Lee, 35, Denver, Colorado, USA. American

CADMAN, William Martin, 32, London, England. British

CAFFARONE, Fabiana, 28, London, England. Argentinian

CAFFARONE, Hernan, 28, London, England. Argentinian

CANADY, Valerie, 25, Morgantown, West Virginia, USA. American

CAPASSO, Gregory, 21, Brooklyn, New York, USA. American

CARDWELL, Timothy Michael, 21, Cresco, Pennsylvania, USA. American

CARLSSON, Bernt Wilmar, 50, New York City, USA. Swedish

CAWLEY, Richard Anthony, 43, New York City, USA. American

CIULLA, Frank, 45, Parkridge, New Jersey, USA. American

COHEN, Theodora Eugenia, 20, Long Island, New York, USA. American

COKER, Eric Michael, 20, Mendham, New Jersey, USA. American

COKER, Jason Michael, 20, Mendham, New Jersey, USA. American

COLASANTI, Gary Leonard, 20, Melrose, Massachusetts, USA. American

CONCANNON, Thomas, 51, Banbury, England. Irish

CONCANNON, Bridget, 53, Banbury, England. Irish

CONCANNON, Sean, 16, Banbury, England. British

CORNER, Tracey Jane, 17, Millhouses, Sheffield, England. British

CORY, Scott, 20, Old Lyme, Connecticut, USA. American

COURSEY, Willis Larry, 40, San Antonio, Texas, USA. American

COYLE, Patricia Mary, 20, Wallingford, Connecticut, USA. American

CUMNOCK, John Binning, 38, Coral Gables, Florida, USA. American

CURRY, Joseph Patrick, 31, Fort Devens, Massachusetts, USA. American

DANIELS, William Allan, 40, Belle Mead, New Jersey, USA. American

DATER, Gretchen Joyce, 20, Ramsay, New Jersey, USA. American

DAVIS, Shannon, 19, Shelton, Connecticut, USA. American

DELLA-RIPA, Gabriel, 46, Floral Park, New York, USA. Italian

DIMAURO, Joyce Christine, 32, New York City, USA. American

DINARDO, Gianfranca, 26, London, England. Italian

DIX, Peter Thomas Stanley, 35, London, England. Irish

DIXIT, Om, 54, Fairborn, Ohio, USA. Indian

DIXIT, Shanti, 54, Fairborn, Ohio, USA. Indian

DORNSTEIN, David Scott, 25, Philadelphia, Pennsylvania, USA. American

DOYLE, Michael Joseph, 30, Voorhees, New Jersey, USA. American

EGGLESTON, Edgar Howard III, 24, Glens Falls, New York, USA. American

ERGIN, Turhan, 27, West Hartford, Connecticut, USA. American

FISHER, Charles Thomas IV, 34, London, England. American

FLICK, Clayton Lee, 25, Coventry, England. British

FLYNN, John Patrick, 21, Montville, New Jersey, USA. American

FONDILER, Arthur, 33, West Armonk, New York, USA. American

FORTUNE, Robert Gerard, 40, Jackson Heights, New York, USA. American

FREEMAN, Paul Matthew Stephen, 25, London, England. Canadian

FULLER, James Ralph, 50, Bloomfield Hills, Michigan, USA. American

GABOR, Ibolya Robertne, 79, Budapest, Hungary. Hungarian

GALLAGHER, Amy Beth, 22, Quebec, Canada. American

GANNON, Matthew Kevin, 34, North Ardmore, California, USA. American

GARCZYNSKI, Kenneth Raymond, 37, North Brunswick, New Jersey, USA. American

GIBSON, Kenneth James, 20, New York, USA. American

GIEBLER, William David, 29, London, England. American

GORDON, Olive Leonora, 25, London, England. British

GORDON-GORGACZ, Linda Susan, 39, London, England. American

GORGACZ, Anne Madelene, 76, Newcastle, Pennsylvania, USA. American

GORGACZ, Lorette Anne, 47, Newcastle, Pennsylvania, USA. American

GOULD, David, 45, Pittsburgh, Pennsylvania, USA. American

GUERVORGIAN, André Nikolai, 32, Long Island, New York, USA. French

HALL, Nicola Jane, 23, Sandton, South Africa. Australian

HALSCH, Lorraine Frances, 31, Fairport, New York, USA. American

HARTUNIAN, Lynne Carol, 21, Schenectady, New York, USA. American

HAWKINS, Anthony Lacey, 57, Brooklyn, New York, USA. British

HERBERT, Pamela Elaine, 19, Battle Creek, Michigan, USA. American

HILBERT, Rodney Peter, 40, Newton, Pennsylvania, USA. American

HILL, Alfred, 29, Sonthofen, West Germany. West German

HOLLISTER, Katherine Augusta, 20, Rego Park, New York, USA. American

HUDSON, Josephine Mary, 22, London, England. British

HUDSON, Sophie Ailette Miriam, 26, Paris, France. French

HUDSON, Melina, 16, Albany, New York, USA. American

HUNT, Karen Lee, 20, Webster, New York, USA. American

HURST, Roger Elwood, 38, Ringwood, New Jersey, USA. American

IVELL, Elizabeth Sophie, 19, Robertsbridge, East Sussex, England. British

JAAFAR, Khaled Nazir, 20, Dearborn, Michigan, USA. Lebanese/American

JECK, Robert van Houten, 57, Mountain Lakes, New Jersey, USA. American

JEFFREYS, Paul Avron, 36, Kingston-upon-Thames, Surrey, England. British

JEFFREYS, Rachel, 23, Kingston-upon-Thames, Surrey, England. British

JERMYN, Kathleen Mary, 20, Staten Island, New York, USA. American

JOHNSON, Beth Ann, 21, Greenburg, Pennsylvania, USA. American

JOHNSON, Mary Alice Lincoln, 25, Wayland, Massachusetts, USA. American

JOHNSON, Timothy Baron, 21, Neptune Township, New Jersey, USA. American

JONES, Christopher Andrew, 20, Claverack, New York, USA. American

KELLY, Julianne Frances, 20, Dedham, Massachusetts, USA. American

KINGHAM, Jay Joseph, 44, Potomac, Maryland, USA. American

KLEIN, Patricia Ann, 35, Trenton, New Jersey, USA. American

KOSMOWSKI, Gregory, 40, Milford, Michigan, USA. American

KULUKUNDIS, Minas Christopher, 38, London, England. British

LARIVIERE, Ronald Albert, 33, Alexandria, Virginia, USA. American

LECKBURG, Robert Milton, 30, Piscataway, New Jersey, USA. American

LEYRER, William Chase, 46, Bay Shore, New York, USA. American

LINCOLN, Wendy Anne, 23, North Adams, Massachusetts, USA. American

LOWENSTEIN, Alexander Silas, 21, Morristown, New Jersey, USA. American

LUDLOW, Lloyd David, 41, New York City, USA. American

LURBKE, Maria Theresia, 25, Balve Beckhum, West Germany. West German

MCALLISTER, William John, 26, Sunbury-on-Thames, Middlesex, England. British

MCCARTHY, Daniel Emmet, 31, Brooklyn, New York, USA. American

MCCOLLUM, Robert Eugene, 61, Wayne, Pennsylvania, USA. American

MACK, William Edward, 30, New York City, USA. American

McKEE, Charles Dennis, 40, Arlington, Virginia, USA. American

McLAUGHLIN, Bernard Joseph, 30, Bristol, England. American

MALICOTE, Douglas Eugene, 22, New York City, USA. American

MALICOTE, Wendy Gay, 21, Mannheim, West Germany. American

MAREK, Elizabeth Lillian, 30, New York City, USA. American

MARENGO, Louis Anthony, 33, Rochester, Michigan, USA. American

MARTIN, Noel George, 27, Clapton, London, England. Jamaican

MASLOWSKI, Diane Maria, 30, New York City, USA. American

MELBER, Jane Susan, 27, Burnt Oak, Middlesex, England. American

MERRILL, John, 35, Baldock, Hertfordshire, England. British

MIAZGA, Suzanne Marie, 22, Marcy, New York, USA. American

MILLER, Joseph Kenneth, 56, Woodmere, New York, USA. American

MITCHELL, Jewel Courtney, 32, Brooklyn, New York, USA. Guyanese

MONETTI, Richard Paul, 20, Cherry Hill, New Jersey, USA. American

MORGAN, Jane Ann, 37, London, England. American

MORSON, Eva Ingeborg, 48, New York City, USA. West German

Mosey, Helga Rachael, 19, Warley, West Midlands, England. British

Mulroy, Ingrid Elizabeth, 25, Lund, Sweden. Swedish

Mulroy, John, 59, East Northport, New York, USA. Irish

Mulroy, Sean Kevin, 25, Lund, Sweden. American

Noonan, Karen Elizabeth, 20, Potomac, Maryland, USA. American

O'Connor, Daniel Emmett, 31, Dorchester, Massachusetts, USA. American

O'Neil, Mary Denice, 21, Bronx, New York, USA. American

Otenasek, Anne Lindsey, 21, Baltimore, Maryland, USA. American

Owen, Bryony Elise, 1, Easton, Bristol, England. British

Owen, Gwyneth Yvonne Margaret, 29, Easton, Bristol, England. British

Owens, Laura Abigail, 8, Cherry Hill, New Jersey, USA. American

Owens, Martha, 44, Cherry Hill, New Jersey, USA. American

Owens, Robert Plack, 45, Cherry Hill, New Jersey, USA. American

Owens, Sarah Rebecca, 14, Cherry Hill, New Jersey, USA. American

Pagnucco, Robert Italo, 51, South Salem, New York, USA. American

Papadopolous, Christos Michael, 45, Lawrence, New York, USA. Greek/American

Peirce, Peter Raymond, 40, Perrysburgh, Ohio, USA. American

PESCATORE, Michael, 33, Solon, Ohio, USA. American

PHILIPPS, Sarah Suzannah Buchanan, 20, Newtonville, Massachusetts, USA. American

PHILLIPS, Frederick Sandford, 27, Little Rock, Arkansas, USA. American

PITT, James Andrew Campbell, 24, South Hadley, Massachusetts, USA. American

PLATT, David, 33, Staten Island, New York, USA. American

PORTER, Walter Leonard, 35, Brooklyn, New York, USA. American

POSEN, Pamela Lynn, 20, Harrison, New York, USA. American

PUGH, William, 56, Margate, New Jersey, USA. American

QUIGUYAN, Crisostomo Estrella, 43, Wembley, London, England. Filipino

RAMSES, Rajesh Tarsis Priskel, 35, Leicester, England. Indian

RATTAN, Anmol, 2, Warren, Michigan, USA. American

RATTAN, Garima, 29, Warren, Michigan, USA. Indian

RATTAN, Suruchi, 3, Warren, Michigan, USA. American

REEVES, Anita Lynn, 24, Laurel, Maryland, USA. American

REIN, Mark Alan, 44, New York City, USA. American

RENCEVICZ, Diane Marie, 21, Burlington, New Jersey, USA. American

ROGERS, Louise Ann, 21, Olney, Maryland, USA. American

ROLLER, Edina, 5, Hungary. Hungarian

ROLLER, Janus Gabor, 29, Hungary. Hungarian

ROLLER, Zsuzsana, 27, Hungary. Hungarian

ROOT, Hanne Maria, 26, Toronto, Ontario, Canada. Canadian

ROSEN, Saul Mark, 35, Morris Plains, New Jersey, USA. American

ROSENTHAL, Daniel Peter, 20, Staten Island, New York, USA. American

ROSENTHAL, Andrea Victoria, 22, New York City, USA. American

RUBIN, Arnaud David, 28, Waterloo, Belgium. Belgian

SARACENI, Elyse Jeanne, 20, East London, England. American

SAUNDERS, Scott Christopher, 21, Macungie, Pennsylvania, USA. American

SAUNDERS, Theresa Elizabeth, 28, Sunbury-on-Thames, Middlesex, England. British

SCHAUBLE, Johannes Otto, 41, Kappellenweg, West Germany. West German

SCHLAGETER, Robert Thomas, 20, Rhode Island, USA. American

SCHULTZ, Thomas Britton, 20, Ridgefield, Connecticut, USA. American

SCOTT, Sally Elizabeth, 22, Huntington, New York, USA. British

SHAPIRO, Amy Elizabeth, 21, Stamford, Connecticut, USA. American

SHASTRI, Mridula, 24, Oxford, England. Indian

SHEANSHANG, Joan, 46, New York, USA. American

SIGAL, Irving Stanley, 35, Pennington, New Jersey, USA. American

SIMPSON, Martin Bernard Christopher, 52, Brooklyn, New York, USA. South African

SMITH, Cynthia Joan, 21, Milton, Massachusetts, USA. American

SMITH, Ingrid Anita, 31, Bray, Berkshire, England. British

SMITH, James Alvin, 55, New York, USA. American

SMITH, Mary Edna, 34, New York, USA. American

STEVENSON, Geraldine Anne, 37, Esher, Surrey, England. British

STEVENSON, Hannah Louise, 10, Esher, Surrey, England. British

STEVENSON, John Charles, 38, Esher, Surrey, England. British

STEVENSON, Rachael, 8, Esher, Surrey, England. British

STINNETT, Charlotte Ann, 36, New York City, USA. American

STINNETT, Michael Gary, 26, Duncanville, Texas, USA. American

STINNETT, Stacey Leeanne, 9, Duncanville, Texas, USA. American

STOW, James Ralph, 49, New York City, USA. American

STRATIS, Elia G., 43, Montvale, New Jersey, USA. Sudanese

SWAN, Anthony Selwyn, 29, Brooklyn, New York, USA. Trinidadian

SWIRE, Flora Macdonald Margaret, 24, London, England. British

TAGER, Marc Alex, 22, Hendon, London, England. British

TANAKA, Hidekazu, 26, London, England. Japanese

TERAN, Andrew Alexander, 20, New Haven, Connecticut, USA. British/Bolivian

THOMAS, Arva Anthony, 17, Detroit, Michigan, USA. American

THOMAS, Jonathan Ryan, 2 months, Southfield, Michigan, USA. American

THOMAS, Lawanda, 21, Southfield, Michigan, USA. American

TOBIN, Mark Lawrence, 21, Hempstead, New York, USA. American

TRIMMER-SMITH, David William, 51, New York City, USA. British

TSAIRIS, Alexia Kathryn, 20, Franklyn Lakes, New Jersey, USA. American

VALENTINO, Barry Joseph, 28, San Francisco, California, USA. American

VAN-TIENHOVEN, Thomas Floro, 45, Buenos Aires, Argentina. American

VEJDANY, Asaad Eidi, 46, South Great Neck, New York, USA. Iranian

VRENIOS, Nicholas Andreas, 20, Washington, D.C., USA. American

VULCU, Peter, 21, Alliance, Ohio, USA. Romanian

WAIDO, Janina Jozefa, 61, Chicago, Illinois, USA. Polish

WALKER, Thomas Edwin, 47, Quincy, Massachusetts, USA. American

WEEDON, Kesha, 20, Bronx, New York, USA. American

WESTON, Jerome Lee, 45, Long Island, New York, USA. American

WHITE, Jonathan, 33, North Hollywood, California, USA. American

WILLIAMS, Bonnie Leigh, 21, New York City, USA. American

WILLIAMS, Brittany Luby, 2 months, New York City, USA. American

WILLIAMS, Eric Jon, 24, New York City, USA. American

WILLIAMS, George Waterson, 24, Joppa, Maryland, USA. American

WILLIAMS, Stephanie Leigh, 1, New York City, USA. American

WOLFE, Miriam Luby, 20, Severna Park, Maryland, USA. American

WOODS, Chelsea Marie, 10 months, Vogelweh Housing, West Germany. American

WOODS, Dedera Lynn, 27, Vogelweh Housing, West Germany. American

WOODS, Joe Nathan, 28, Vogelweh Housing, West Germany. American

WOODS, Joe Nathan Jr., 2, Vogelweh Housing, West Germany. American

WRIGHT, Andrew Christopher Gillies, 24, Mitcham, Surrey, England. British

ZWYNEBURG, Mark James, 29, West Nyack, New York, USA. American.

BRITISH RESIDENTS OF LOCKERBIE

FLANNIGAN, Joanne, 10.
FLANNIGAN, Kathleen Mary, 41.
FLANNIGAN, Thomas Brown, 44.
HENRY, Dora Henrietta, 56.
HENRY, Maurice Peter, 63.
LANCASTER, Mary, 81.

MURRAY, Jean Aitken, 82.
SOMERVILLE, John, 40.
SOMERVILLE, Lyndsey Ann, 10.
SOMERVILLE, Paul, 13.
SOMERVILLE, Rosaleen Later, 40.

PAN AM:
QUESTIONS AND SOME
ANSWERS

The following is a list of questions that I submitted to Jeffrey F. Kriendler, Vice President of Corporate Communications for Pan American World Airways Inc., on March 22, 1989, asking for "the fullest replies you feel able to give." Following each question is the answer (in italic) received—or not, as the case may be—from Mr. Kriendler in a letter dated April 27, 1989.

Q. When was Pan Am first made aware by relevant authority of the terrorist cell uncovered by the German BKA in Frankfurt on October 27?

A. *10 November 1988.*

Q. Were the security bulletins of November 2, 4, 17, and December 5 issued to Pan Am, and if so, where and in what form? Did Pan Am receive any other warnings apart from these after the October 26 raid?

A. *Pan Am did not receive any bulletins dated November 2, 14, 17 or December 5 from any source. However, Pan Am received bulletins from various sources.*

Q. What steps were taken by Pan Am, and when, to counter any threats outlined in bulletins the airline received?

A. *[No answer]*

Q. By 21 December 1988 was it still the practice of Pan Am to X-ray only the luggage of non-American and German nationals starting their journey in Frankfurt?

A. *It was not the practice of Pan Am to X-ray only the luggage of non-American and German nationals starting their journey in Frankfurt.*

Q. By the same date, was it the practice of Pan Am not to X-ray luggage of U.K. passengers starting their journey at Heathrow?

A. *It was not the practice of Pan Am to X-ray only the luggage of non-American and United Kingdom nationals starting their journey in London.*

Q. Can you confirm that Pan Am in 1986 applied to the Federal Aviation Administration to increase one-way ticket prices by five dollars to pay for increased security measures?

A. *In 1986, Pan Am and other airlines charged a security surcharge to offset, in part, higher security charges being levied by European airport authorities and governments.*

Q. If this was the case, what additional security measures were undertaken that required this extra money?

A. *[No answer]*

Q. Was Pan Am's Frankfurt Station Manager, H. Leuniger, responsible for security in addition to his other duties?

A. *[No answer]*

Q. If so, is there not a conflict of interest in making the same person responsible for the prompt departure of flights and security?

A. *[No answer]*

Q. Why is Mr. Leuniger no longer in Pan Am's employment?

A. *Mr. Leuniger elected to take early retirement in 1987 but was asked to remain an additional year and did so. His determination to take early retirement, which was to be effective, and indeed was effective, 31 December 1988, was made long before the crash of Flight 103 and had nothing to do with it.*

Q. How much of the luggage, if any, of the transfer passengers who boarded Flight 103 at Frankfurt from other flights was X-rayed?

A. *The checked bags of all interline passengers were X-rayed.*

Q. Are TNA machines available to Pan Am at either Frankfurt or Heathrow, and if so, were they used on any of the Flight 103 luggage?

A. *No.*

Q. On December 21 why was Flight 103 late in leaving London, and by exactly how long was the departure delayed?

A. *Flight 103 on 21 December 1988 was on time.*

Q. Is it the general principle that Pan Am pilots are in overall charge of the security of their planes?

A. *[No answer]*

Q. If so, what facilities are available to them if they are not for some reason happy with the flight?

A. *[No answer]*

Q. Was Captain MacQuarrie aware of the heightened security situation around the time in West Germany, and if so, how was he informed and in what detail?

A. *[No answer]*

Q. Was Pan Am Flight 103 fully booked at any time on December 21?

A. *No.*

Q. Did Pan Am offer discounted tickets on Flight 103, and if so, is that normal practice?

A. *Pan Am did not deviate from its normal ticketing procedure with respect to Flight 103 and did not offer specially discounted tickets for Flight 103.*

Q. Were there any passengers intending to fly Flight 103 who canceled their reservations or transferred to other airlines?

A. *Some passengers canceled or transferred to other airlines or to other Pan Am flights. Likewise, some passengers from other airlines, or scheduled on other Pan Am flights, changed their reservations so as to fly on Flight 103.*

Q. What procedures did Pan Am adopt for handling the aftermath of the disaster?

A. *Pan Am established command posts in New York, London, Frankfurt, Lockerbie, and Carlisle.*

Q. Why was Pan Am reluctant to supply the State Department with a list of the next-of-kin of Flight 103 victims, as testified by a State Department official at the Senate Appropriation's transport subcommittee hearing on March 14?

A. *Pan Am was not reluctant to supply the State Department with a list of the next-of-kin.*

Q. Are you happy with the conduct the members of your staff allocated to families of victims of Flight 103?

A. *Yes.*

Q. How would you respond to Mr. and Mrs. Joe Tobin of Long Island, New York, who say that, in one of the very few conversations they've had with their representative, she said she really didn't want to do the job and had asked to be taken off and then, in return, had been given an extra two families to deal with?

A. *[No answer]*

Q. Is Pan Am satisfied with the assistance given to it, particularly by the U.S. State Department, in dealing with the aftermath of Lockerbie?

A. *It was a very difficult situation, and many organizations and governments expended considerable time, energy, and funds to cope with it.*

Q. Why were Pan Am officials at first reluctant to comply with relatives' wishes to go to Lockerbie?

A. *We believed that since there were no survivors, it was not in the families' best interests.*

Q. Why in Pan Am's 10K for last year is there no provision for spending on security?

A. *[No answer]*

Q. Who in the corporation is in overall charge of security and at what level is he in the structure?

A. *Edward Cunningham, Managing Director, Corporate Security.*

Q. What steps, if any, were taken to improve security following the report prepared for Pan Am by Isaac Yeffet in 1986?

A. *[No answer]*

Q. Would Pan Am consider implementing El Al–style security, with complete hand searching of luggage and their questionnaires?

A. *[No answer]*

Q. How would Pan Am counter the view expressed by Mr. Yeffet that, in common with most other airlines, Pan Am is totally vulnerable to terrorist attack, even after the events of December 21?

A. *[No answer]*

Q. Does Pan Am have any intention of compensating relatives of the disaster victims at levels in excess of those laid down by the Warsaw Convention?

A. *[No answer]*

Q. Does Pan Am consider that the Warsaw Convention, designed prewar to protect "fledgling airlines," is still valid in these days of mass air travel?

A. *The Warsaw Convention is a multilateral treaty ratified by virtually every nation. As such, it is the supreme law of the United States and virtually ever [sic] nation.*

Q. Bearing in mind the threats of subpoenas, how prepared is Pan Am to cooperate with the various congressional committees looking into aspects of the disaster?

A. *Pan Am has consistently cooperated with government authorities in the United States and abroad.*

Q. Does Pan Am support the relatives' groups' call for an independent inquiry into Flight 103?

A. *There are presently inquiries by various governmental agencies and legislative bodies in the United States, the United Kingdom, Scotland, and West Germany.*

Q. At 7:03 P.M. on December 21, if normal procedures were being followed, what would be happening on the flight?

A. *[No answer]*

Q. What was the dinner menu?

A. *[No answer]*

Q. What is the name and address of the passenger who turned up too late to catch the flight? Why was his luggage carried on the flight without him?

A. *[No answer]*

Q. Is it still the practice of Pan Am to hold luggage and cargo for twenty-four hours before flying it without X-raying or searching it?

A. *[No answer]*

Q. When was Pan Am first alerted to the December 5 Helsinki warning and what steps were taken?

A. *On or about 7 December 1988.*

Q. When was Pan Am informed of the December 10 decision of the FAA and the State Department that the December 5 warning was "not credible," and what reaction did that information, if indeed you received it, produce from Pan Am in terms of security measures undertaken at Frankfurt?

A. *About one week after the notice.*

This poem, by the father of twin sons killed at Lockerbie, first appeared in the first edition of the relatives' group newsletter.

To the Editor:
Please print,
*   these the cries of anguish*
My sons are dead
*   dead when I awake*
*   dead when I fall asleep*
*   dead during the day*
*   dead at night*
*   dead.*
I see my sons flung from the heavens side by side
*   colored fluttering hail slamming into*
*   soft Scottish pasture.*
I can no longer look into the heavens.
I see my sons in body bags
*   bones shattered, skulls crushed, faces obliterated,*
*   flesh macerated*
*   unrecognizable, unbearable*
*   identifiable only by tattoos.*
I see soft Scottish pasture pocked with holes
*   emptiness*
*   my sons' mark on the world.*
I see fine young Scotsmen slogging through a grim harvest
*   soulless bodies*
*   dead dreams.*
I see pecuniary pollution
*   fouled suffering*
*   fouled consolation.*

I see my sons sacrificed on an altar of evil
    without mercy
    without honor
    without dignity
    without apology.
And you, Mr. Reagan and Mr. Shultz, may God let you
    see what I see.
And you Mr. Plaskett and Mr. Alpert, may God let you
    see what I see.
And you, the murderers of my sons, may God cleanse your
souls
    and forgive you.

Thomas G. Coker
Father of Jason and Eric Coker

POSTSCRIPT

By early June 1989 police were working on the theory that the bomb was carried onto the plane at Frankfurt by one of two twenty-year-old students who had been studying at a college in Vienna, Austria.

Patricia Coyle of Connecticut, and her friend, Karen Noonan of Maryland, were coming home for Christmas from their course, part of their university studies. Scottish detectives now believe that the PFLP-GC duped the girls into carrying the bomb in their luggage in their classic style: asking them to mail it as a Christmas present to a friend in the USA.

As the book goes to press, it is not clear whether the students were given the device in Vienna or in West Germany after flying from the Austrian capital to join Flight 103.

GLOSSARY

AAIB: The Air Accident Investigation Branch of the U.K. Department of Transport

BKA: Bundes Kriminal Amt; the West German federal police force

CIA: Central Intelligence Agency; the United States Department of International Intelligence operations

CID: Criminal Investigation Department; the plainclothes branch of U.K. police forces

FAA: The Federal Aviation Administration; the U.S. body responsible for the regulation of the airline industry

PFLP-GC: Popular Front for the Liberation of Palestine–General Command; the Palestinian terror group that broke away from the PLO in 1986

PLO: Palestine Liberation Organization; the main organization, based in Tunis and headed by Yasir Arafat, campaigning for a Palestinian homeland. The PLO has now renounced violence.

INDEX